emily cier

color, block & quilt

Copyright © 2012 by Emily Cier

All rights reserved. No part of this work may be reproduced, distributed, or transmitted in any form or by any means, including photocopying, recording, or other electronic or mechanical methods, without prior written permission from the author.

Permission is granted to craft items and photocopy the templates on p. 31 for personal use only.

Printed in the United States of America

First Printing, 2012

ISBN 978-1481050135

www.CarolinaPatchworks.com

acknowledgments

Sean. For being there.

Maeve. For the color pink.

Liam. For the colors blue and purple.

Robert Kaufman Fabrics. For making and providing box after box of glorious Kona Cotton for the quilts.

Angela Walters. For every perfect stitch, swirl, doodle and circle.

The State of Washington. For being so amazingly beautiful.

Table of Contents

5	Introduction		
6	HOW TO		
6	Color, Block & Quilt	10	Combinations
7	How Many Quilts ...	14	Quilting Gallery
8	Sewing Basics and Tips	29	Half-Square Triangle
9	What's in a Name?	30	Quarter Curve
32	COLOR		
36	COLOR 101: terra	40	COLOR 109: luma
36	COLOR 102: circum	40	COLOR 110: omni
37	COLOR 103: eco	41	COLOR 111: paleo
37	COLOR 104: aqua	41	COLOR 112: nano
38	COLOR 105: geo	42	COLOR 113: inter
38	COLOR 106: super	42	COLOR 114: lapis
39	COLOR 107: trans	43	COLOR 115: lux
39	COLOR 108: florus		
44	BLOCK		
46	BLOCK 101: -orbis	62	BLOCK 109: -tele
48	BLOCK 102: -flora	64	BLOCK 110: -retro
50	BLOCK 103: -rumpo	66	BLOCK 111: -insta
52	BLOCK 104: -pluvia	68	BLOCK 112: -proto
54	BLOCK 105: -loco	70	BLOCK 113: -curva
56	BLOCK 106: -auto	72	BLOCK 114: -parallel
58	BLOCK 107: -domus	74	BLOCK 115: -codex
60	BLOCK 108: -macro		
76	QUILT		
78	QUILT 101: -cosm	100	QUILT 106: -scope
82	QUILT 102: -ruption	104	QUILT 107: -athon
86	QUILT 103: -esque	110	QUILT 108: -ism
92	QUILT 104: -mania	114	QUILT 109: -ette
96	QUILT 105: -asaurus	118	QUILT 110: -avore
122	APPENDIX A: I Want That Exact Quilt		
124	omni-retro-cosm	134	aqua-codex-athon
125	terra-pluvia-scope	135	florus-orbis-athon
126	super-auto-loco-ruption	136	lapis-curva-ism
128	eco-parallel-esque	137	inter-proto-ism
129	paleo-domus-esque	138	lux-curva-ette
130	geo-macro-flora-mania	139	nano-poly-ette
131	luma-tele-asaurus	140	circum-poly-avore
132	trans-poly-asaurus		
142	APPENDIX B: Where in Washington		
144	About the Author		
146	Resources		

Introduction

Quilts, to me, are about two things: color and shape. Sure, there's more than that — pattern, texture, tradition, technique. And beneath that — community, ideas, beauty, expression, warmth. But ultimately it all comes back to color and shape, and how they interact to form an endlessly rich set of quilts, each unique, each personal. This book is my attempt to take a journey through the possibilities presented by that simple idea, and to share that journey with you — and perhaps, at the same time, help you see the world of quilting in a different light.

So here's the deal. This book contains three elements: color palettes, blocks, and quilts. Each is straightforward in its own right, and it's up to you to pick one color palette, one quilt, and as many blocks as fit in that quilt. But that's where the straight and forward end, as the path you pick will lead you to a different quilt than any other reader of this book. Think of it as discovery: finding a tiny, beautiful jewel all your own in an endless field of color, and shape. Because that's how I see the world of quilts, and that's the field I wander through each time I sit down to create a new design. Enjoy your journey, and I hope you find something I've never dreamed of!

HOW TO: Color, Block & Quilt

COLOR, BLOCK & QUILT takes the basic three elements of a quilt and breaks them down so you can mix and match to your heart's content, making a quilt that is all your own that fits your needs, space and schedule.

Step 1. Pick Your Colors.

What kind of mood are you in today?

- It's the dead of winter and you're looking for something to brighten up your day as you head to spring.
- Your son or husband wants a quilt but doesn't want florals and froof!
- The baby shower is tomorrow and you haven't even started on the little bundle of joy's new quilt.
- You've decided to finally make a quilt just for you. Schedule be damned. This one is going to rock.

The COLOR section (pp. 32-43) is here to inspire. Most of my color inspiration comes from the world around me and most notably large, expansive landscapes and up-close macro photography of flowers.

While the final palette may not always match the colors in the photo 100%, it keeps the overall feeling of color that the photo inspires.

All of the palettes (and blocks and quilts) in this book are built from Robert Kaufman's Kona Cotton Solids (see *Resources*, p. 146), a collection of 243 distinct tones.

Once you have chosen your palette, it's time to pick blocks.

Sometimes you have to go back and forth between the steps to finalize your plan. That's okay. Stick with it.

Before you can finalize block picks, you need to know how many blocks and in what sizes you'll need. So approach the next two sections together.

Step 2. Pick Your Blocks.

What is this project all about?

- Do you want to use one block style for the entire quilt?
- Do you want to use a different block style in every spot?
- Are you comfortable sewing curves?
- What is your schedule like? Are you ok with sewing 12 large time consuming blocks for a bed sized quilt?

The first thing to decide is one block style vs. two block styles vs. lots of block styles. I love the simplicity that one single block in multiple sizes and different rotations lends the overall design. But on the other hand, I love the traditional, sampler look of every block being different (think block swaps!), but still linked together in color.

Once you have a rough idea of the blocks for your quilt, it's time to think about what you're going to be doing with these blocks!

Step 3. Pick Your Quilt.

Where is this quilt going?

- If it's headed to the wall or to a baby shower, the larger bed-sized quilts would probably be a bad idea.
- If you have a king bed and are hankering for a new bed quilt, you should probably head straight for the larger quilts.

Like a quilt but want it in a different size? Check out the suggestions in QUILT, p. 76, for ideas on how to transform your favorite quilt into the size you need.

Step 4. Finalize Your Choices.

Once you have your quilt choice finalized, go back and visit the blocks. Do you still like the block(s) you picked in the context of your chosen quilt? Do you want to add more block styles? Take any away?

Once you have your quilt and block choices finalized, go back and visit the color. Does it still all work together?

Step 5. Make Your Color Plan.

If your quilt has a small frame around the blocks, make sure the border color isn't in any part of the block that will touch the border. Also, you don't have to use every color in the palette in every block. It's ok for some colors to only be in one block.

Having a hard time figuring out what to put where? The COLOR, BLOCK & QUILT: WORKBOOK (see *Resources*, p. 146) can provide a great space to plan your colors, blocks and quilt.

Step 6. Make Your Quilt.

Ready! Set! Go! Remember, these quilts can be as easy (small quilt and easy blocks) or difficult (big quilt and difficult blocks) as you want them to be. So make your choices and have fun!

How Many Quilts Could a Quilter Quilt if a Quilter Read Color, Block & Quilt?

We all know about the exalted uniqueness of the proverbial snowflake. Some of the beauty of a silent midwinter blizzard springs from the almost oppressive quantity of individuality suffusing the tiny particles of snow, each destined to be fundamentally different not only from its neighbors but from every other flake ever to have formed or ever to form. Tiny variations in temperature, humidity, and pressure nudge the growth of ice crystals gently into one of a myriad of combinations so vast that merely computing their number would stymie the most determined effort, thrusting them from their chemically simple and imperceivably insignificant origins to the realm of legend by virtue of simple innumeracy.

Snowflakes have nothing on quilts.

Start with a choice of color palette. Multiply by the number of quilt designs available to be paired with it. 150 possibilities so far; paltry. But that's just 2 decisions. Next, pick a block from among the 15 choices. Now pick another. And another. For some quilts, you need to pick 3 or 4; others, 11 or 12. We're up to more than a dozen decisions already. How many quilt combinations do you think are possible so far? Go on, guess.

Wrong.

2,206,264,748,501,250.

Two quadrillion, two hundred six trillion, two hundred sixty four billion, seven hundred forty eight million, five hundred one thousand, two hundred and fifty.

I almost hate to point out that we haven't even thought about how to apply the color palette: which colors to use for which elements of each block and the quilt itself. Another few dozen decisions. Smaller ones, to be sure, but different choices will still result in quilts that look quite distinct from one another.

Factor those in, and: 4.846×10^{75}. Rounding up, that's a five with 75 zeroes. That number doesn't even have a name, though we could perhaps refer to it as a nonillion times a quattuordecillion. Times five.

Beat that, snowflakes.

HOW TO:
Sewing Basics and Tips

While all of the projects in this book follow the basic quilting routine — choosing colors, making blocks, assembling the quilt, and finishing — here are some basic sewing tips to help you along the way.

Do I need any special quilting tools?
The projects in this book don't require any specialty tools beyond your basic quilting supplies. If you are planning on projects with Quarter Curves, you'll need to trace or photocopy the templates on p. 31. The following are some basic tools I find handy:
- 24" × 36" cutting mat
- Rotary cutter and extra blades: if you can't remember the last time you replaced your blade, it's past time to do so.
- 6½" × 24" cutting ruler: my preferred ruler size for long cuts.
- 4½" square cutting ruler: my preferred ruler size for small cuts.
- Sewing tool basket: always right next to my machine with needles, oil, dusting brush, pins, water soluble pen, etc.

Prewashing: Yay or nay?
I prefer not to prewash my fabrics because I feel that the small pieces keep their shapes better when they have not been washed, but it's up to you. Please note that the fabric yardage requirements given for each project do not factor in significant shrinkage due to prewashing.

Cutting Notes
- All cuts assume that the fabric is at least 40˝ wide.
- The yardage requirements include a small amount of extra fabric in case of a cutting error.
- If a piece longer than 40" wide is needed, piece two width-of-fabric (WOF) pieces together, press seams open, then cut the size needed.
- Some longer strips in the projects, such as the 41½" pieces used in QUILT 106, pp. 100-103, may not need to be pieced before cutting depending on the exact width of your fabric.
- If you have one, use a 28mm blade when cutting the Quarter Curve pieces. This smaller blade will make for easier turns.
- Also, when cutting Quarter Curves, don't cut too many layers at once as you end up chopping through the fabrics instead of making a smooth cut. Watch your fingertips and nails!

Piecing Notes
- A ¼" seam allowance is used for all seams in all of the projects. Accuracy is the key to successful piecing and making sure that all pieces of the blocks and quilts stay horizontally and vertically aligned.
- Keep a ruler handy to double-check the length of the pieces as you use them. It's easier to double-check a measurement before you sew the pieces together than having to un-sew and re-sew with the correct pieces.
- A walking foot isn't just for quilting! It can help keep the feed even when piecing even the smallest of seams.
- Make sure not to pull the fabric when pressing,

especially around the edges where waves and distortion can occur.

- Mistakes can happen easily in any quilt. Take your time to make sure you are using the right color, size, placement, and so on. Don't get frustrated if you end up having to un-sew a portion at some point. It will be worth it in the end!
- Using small sticky notes next to the fabric piles (denoting fabric 'A', 'B', etc) can be helpful in keeping track of which fabric is which, especially when using different colors than are shown in the illustrations.

Quilting and Finishing Notes
- Backing fabric should be at least 4" wider than the quilt top on all sides. Piece your backing fabric if necessary, with a ½" seam pressed open.
- Use your batting of choice, making sure it is at least 4" wider than the quilt top on all sides.
- Make your quilt sandwich by laying the backing wrong side up. Top with batting and then the quilt top right side up, making sure it is centered on the backing and batting. Baste with safety pins about 4" apart.
- Before deciding on a quilting design, check the batting manufacturer's specifications regarding the distance between quilting lines.
- Check out the Quilting Gallery on pp. 14-28 for ideas and inspiration on quilting these projects.
- All binding yardage is based on 2½" strips and 40" wide fabric.

What's in a Name?

Naming a quilt is one of the parts of a project I love the most — and dread even more. I took a different approach to the task in this book.

All of the elements needed names — color palettes, blocks, and quilts. As did the finished projects in APPENDIX A: I Want That Exact Quilt (p. 122). It would be nice if, at the same time, I could help you out a bit in naming your unique creation.

As these quilts are built from basic blocks, it seemed appropriate for the names to be built the same way. So I went back to the Latin roots of building words with a little inspiration from my son's beloved Tyrannosaurus Rex, which aptly means "tyrant lizard."

Each element got a name. When the quilts are assembled, they take on all the names of their respective parts. For example, take a project with the color palette *florus*, using the block called *-pluvia* and set in the quilt *-asaurus*. The finish quilt would be dubbed *florus-pluvia-asaurus*. Or, with a little finessing*, *florapluviasaurus*.

When a quilt has two different blocks, it gets both block names, such as *geo-macro-flora-mania*, p. 130.

When a quilt has more than two blocks, those blocks names are replaced with *poly* ("many"), such as *trans-poly-asaurus*, p. 132.

* When one name ends in a vowel and the next name starts with a vowel, such as pluvia and asaurus, it can be a jumble to get out. You can take out vowels as needed so your quilt could be *florus-pluv-asaurus*. You can do the same with consonant pairs, and even just apply a little poetic license and bubble gum until the name flows to your satisfaction. In this book, just to remove any confusion when you're trying to trace a quilt's ancestry, I didn't remove letters.

HOW TO: sewing basics and tips

HOW TO: Combinations

All these possibilities can be a bit daunting. Where do you start? This section has some examples showing how you might figure out where you are, what you want, and how to get there.

circum-poly-ette: BABY SHOWER

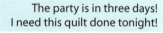

The party is in three days! I need this quilt done tonight!

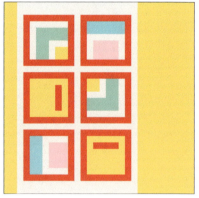

Color

It's a girl but I don't want it to be stereotypically pink but I also still want it to be feminine. Let's go with...

circum, COLOR 102, p. 36

Block

I need this done tonight so simple blocks might be best. I'm also thinking I'd like 2 or 3 blocks. Let's go with ...

-auto, BLOCK 106, p. 56
-insta, BLOCK 111, p. 66
-parallel, BLOCK 114, p. 72

Quilt

Since she'll be born in the wintertime, perhaps a small quilt would be best for riding in the car and stroller. Let's go with ...

-ette, QUILT 109, p. 114

luma-tele-mania: ALMOST THE SAME

I love the color and the block in *luma-tele-asaurus* (p. 131), I just want them in a different quilt.

Color
The color is simply divine. Lots of grey to match the cold winter sky but with a pop of bright to remind you that summer isn't too far away. Let's go with...

luma, COLOR 109, p. 40

Block
It's perfect the way it is. We just need to make some in other sizes for the quilt. Let's go with ...

-tele, BLOCK 109, p. 62

Quilt
I loved the one block plus sashing of the original luma-tele-asaurus quilt (p. 131) but want something a little smaller. Let's go with ...

-mania, QUILT 104, p. 92

omni-retro-cosm: RETRO REDUX

I really love *omni-retro-cosm* in Appendix A (p. 124), but I want to mix up the colors.

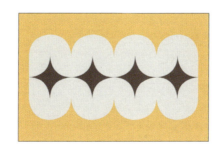

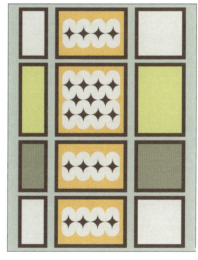

Color
I really love the color palette, I just want to mix them up a little bit! Let's stick with...

omni, COLOR 110, p. 40

Block
Perfect! With some color switching of course. Let's stick with ...

-retro, BLOCK 110, p. 64

Quilt
Same as the blocks! Switch the colors around and you have a whole different quilt. Let's stick with ...

-cosm, QUILT 101, p. 78

lapis-poly-esque: SAMPLER-O-RAMA

I love *-esque* and I want a sampler look with all different blocks.

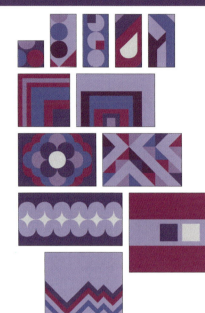

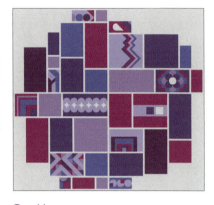

Color

This one is for me and I like purple. LOTS of purple. Let's go with...

lapis, COLOR 114, p. 42

Block

This quilt uses 12 blocks. So we'll start from the beginning of the book and make one of each until I hit 12. Let's go with ...

-orbis, BLOCK 101, p. 46
-flora, BLOCK 102, p. 48
-rumpo, BLOCK 103, p. 50
-pluvia, BLOCK 104, p. 52
-loco, BLOCK 105, p. 54
-auto, BLOCK 106, p. 56
-domus, BLOCK 107, p. 58
-macro, BLOCK 108, p. 60
-tele, BLOCK 109, p. 62
-retro, BLOCK 110, p. 64
-insta, BLOCK 111, p. 66
-proto, BLOCK 112, p. 68

Quilt

It was love at first sight. We'll use a light grey in the background so the purple pops. Let's go with ...

-esque, QUILT 103, p. 86

nano-poly-asaurus: JUST ONE CHANGE FROM APPENDIX A

I love trans-poly-asaurus (p. 132), I just don't love the colors!

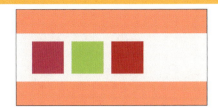

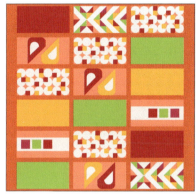

Color
Not everyone loves earthtones. I get it. Let's go with…

nano, COLOR 112, p. 41

Block
It's a great mix. A little sampler with a little order. Let's go with …

-rumpo, BLOCK 103, p. 50
-pluvia, BLOCK 104, p. 52
-tele, BLOCK 109, p. 62
-insta, BLOCK 111, p. 66

Quilt
It will be perfect for snuggling on the couch and the kids' tent-making. Let's go with …

-asaurus, QUILT 105, p. 96

HOW TO: combinations

Quilting Gallery

Once you've finished your top, quilting it can be as simple or as intricate as you choose. An all-over stipple or a round of stitching-in-the-ditch will hold things together and still look classy, but I like to think of quilting as an opportunity to have some fun and add another dimension to the project with some whimsical doodles or patterns that reflect and enhance the quilt's overall design.

The talented Angela Walters handled the quilting for all of the projects in this book, and came up with some pretty imaginative designs that spotlight the focal points in the foreground and the background. At the same time they help the foreground "pop", with patterns in the background quietly emphasizing the shapes in the foreground, flowing around them or echoing them.

This Quilting Gallery highlights Angela's amazing quilting and hopefully provides some inspiration for the quilting part of your project. It's divided into three sections:

- Quilting the Pieced Blocks
- Quilting the Solid Blocks
- Quilting the Quilts

Quilting the Pieced Blocks shows different quilting ideas for the BLOCKS. Most of the blocks have a distinction between foreground and background, and this is important to consider when coming up with your quilting approach. For example, *super-auto-loco-ruption* to the right has a white background with colored 'Y' shapes in the foreground. The quilting emphasizes this with tight swirls across the shapes in the foreground, while in the background simple straight lines highlight the foreground shapes. Quilting can also be used to embellish portions of the block. In *geo-macro-flora-mania* on p. 17, Angela took the abstract floral shapes within -flora, BLOCK 102, as inspiration and quilted floral shapes around and on top of the circles and leaves, making for an amazing combination that reinforced the themes of the design.

Quilting the Solid Blocks shows different quilting ideas for the solid blocks that are in many of the quilt layouts. The large, empty spots are an important part of the overall design of each quilt, but nonetheless benefit from a little seasoning themselves to add interest and compliment the pieced blocks.

Quilting the Quilts shows some ideas for the sashing, borders and background, while still highlighting the blocks.

Before you start, make a quilting plan. This needn't be anything formal, it's just a way to get your own thoughts together so that you don't jump in and then change your mind after a few irreversible minutes of stitching. Sketch, doodle, draw on a steamy mirror while getting ready in the morning — whatever works for you. The COLOR, BLOCK & QUILT: WORKBOOK (see *Resources*, p. 146) can provide a great space not only for planning your quilt, but planning your quilting as well.

For more information on Angela, her quilting, classes and books, I heartily recommend checking out quiltingismytherapy.com.

Quilting the Pieced Blocks

TOP LEFT: **lapis-curva-ism**
lapis, COLOR 114, p. 42
-curva, BLOCK 113, p. 70
-ism, QUILT 108, p. 110
APPENDIX, p. 136

TOP RIGHT: **trans-poly-asaurus**
trans, COLOR 107, p. 39
-rumpo, BLOCK 103, p. 50
-asaurus, QUILT 105, p. 96
APPENDIX, p. 132

BOTTOM LEFT: **super-auto-loco-ruption**
super, COLOR 106, p. 38
-loco, BLOCK 105, p. 54
-ruption, QUILT 102, p. 82
APPENDIX, p. 126

BOTTOM RIGHT: **nano-poly-ette**
nano, COLOR 112, p. 41
-tele, BLOCK 109, p. 62
-codex, BLOCK 115, p. 74
-ette, QUILT 109, p. 114
APPENDIX, p. 139

quilting gallery

TOP LEFT: **inter-proto-ism**
inter, COLOR 113, p. 42
-proto, BLOCK 112, p. 68
-ism, QUILT 108, p. 110
APPENDIX, p. 137

TOP RIGHT: **aqua-codex-athon**
aqua, COLOR 104, p. 37
-codex, BLOCK 115, p. 74
-athon, QUILT 107, p. 104
APPENDIX, p. 134

BOTTOM: **luma-tele-asaurus**
luma, COLOR 109, p. 40
-tele, BLOCK 109, p. 62
-asaurus, QUILT 105, p. 96
APPENDIX, p. 131

color, block & quilt

TOP: **geo-macro-flora-mania**
geo, COLOR 105, p. 38
-flora, BLOCK 102, p. 48
-mania, QUILT 104, p. 92
APPENDIX, p. 130

BOTTOM LEFT: **omni-retro-cosm**
omni, COLOR 110, p. 40
-retro, BLOCK 110, p. 64
-cosm, QUILT 101, p. 78
APPENDIX, p. 124

BOTTOM RIGHT: **trans-poly-asaurus**
trans, COLOR 107, p. 39
-insta, BLOCK 111, p. 66
-asaurus, QUILT 105, p. 96
APPENDIX, p. 132

quilting gallery

TOP LEFT: **eco-parallel-esque**
eco, COLOR 103, p. 37
-parallel, BLOCK 114, p. 72
-esque, QUILT 103, p. 86
APPENDIX, p. 128

TOP RIGHT: **paleo-domus-esque**
paleo, COLOR 111, p. 41
-domus, BLOCK 107, p. 58
-esque, QUILT 103, p. 86
APPENDIX, p. 129

BOTTOM: **super-auto-loco-ruption**
super, COLOR 106, p. 38
-auto, BLOCK 106, p. 56
-ruption, QUILT 102, p. 82
APPENDIX, p. 126

TOP: **florus-orbis-athon**
florus, COLOR 108, p. 39
-orbis, BLOCK 101, p. 46
-athon, QUILT 107, p. 104
APPENDIX, p. 135

BOTTOM LEFT: **trans-poly-asaurus**
trans, COLOR 107, p. 39
-pluvia, BLOCK 104, p. 52
-athon, QUILT 105, p. 96
APPENDIX, p. 132

BOTTOM RIGHT: **geo-macro-flora-mania**
geo, COLOR 105, p. 38
-macro, BLOCK 108, p. 60
-mania, QUILT 104, p. 92
APPENDIX, p. 130

quilting gallery

Quilting the Solid Blocks

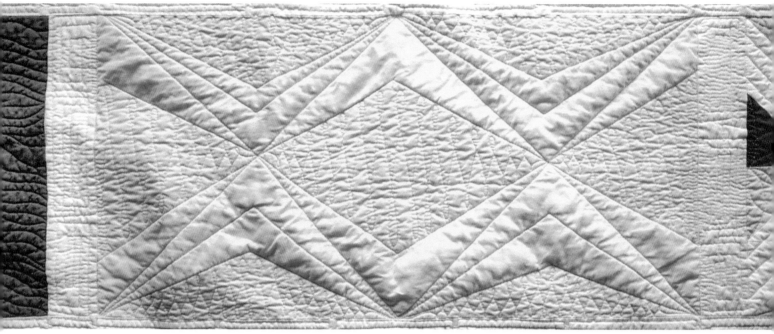

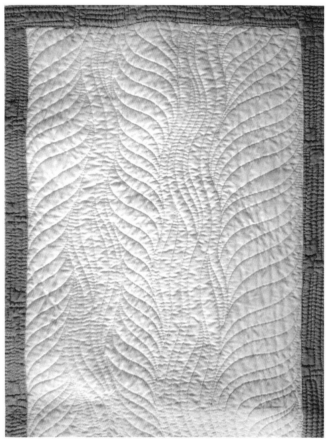

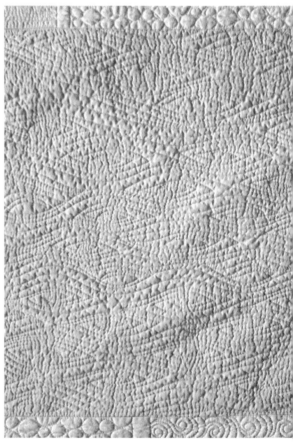

TOP: luma-tele-asaurus
luma, COLOR 109, p. 40
-asaurus, QUILT 105, p. 96
APPENDIX, p. 131

BOTTOM LEFT: paleo-domus-esque
paleo, COLOR 111, p. 41
-esque, QUILT 103, p. 86
APPENDIX, p. 129

BOTTOM RIGHT: eco-parallel-esque
eco, COLOR 103, p. 37
-esque, QUILT 103, p. 86
APPENDIX, p. 128

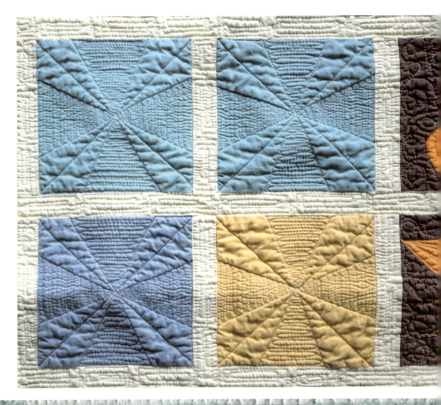

TOP: **terra-pluvia-scope**
terra, COLOR 101, p. 36
-scope, QUILT 106, p. 100
APPENDIX, p. 125

BOTTOM: **eco-parallel-esque**
eco, COLOR 103, p. 37
-esque, QUILT 103, p. 86
APPENDIX, p. 128

quilting gallery

TOP: trans-poly-asaurus
trans, COLOR 107, p. 39
-asaurus, QUILT 105, p. 96
APPENDIX, p. 132

BOTTOM RIGHT: omni-retro-cosm
omni, COLOR 110, p. 40
-cosm, QUILT 101, p. 78
APPENDIX, p. 124

BOTTOM LEFT: paleo-domus-esque
paleo, COLOR 111, p. 41
-esque, QUILT 103, p. 86
APPENDIX, p. 129

TOP LEFT: omni-retro-cosm
omni, COLOR 110, p. 40
-cosm, QUILT 101, p. 78
APPENDIX, p. 124

TOP RIGHT: trans-poly-asaurus
trans, COLOR 107, p. 39
-asaurus, QUILT 105, p. 96
APPENDIX, p. 132

BOTTOM: trans-poly-asaurus
trans, COLOR 107, p. 39
-asaurus, QUILT 105, p. 96
APPENDIX, p. 132

quilting gallery

Quilting the Quilts

TOP LEFT: **luma-tele-asaurus**
luma, COLOR 109, p. 40
-tele, BLOCK 109, p. 62
-asaurus, QUILT 105, p. 96
APPENDIX, p. 131

BOTTOM LEFT: **omni-retro-cosm**
omni, COLOR 110, p. 40
-retro, BLOCK 110, p. 64
-cosm, QUILT 101, p. 78
APPENDIX, p. 124

ABOVE: **florus-orbis-athon**
florus, COLOR 108, p. 39
-orbis, BLOCK 101, p. 46
-athon, QUILT 107, p. 104
APPENDIX, p. 135

TOP: **super-auto-loco-ruption**
super, COLOR 106, p. 38
-auto, BLOCK 105, p. 54
-ruption, QUILT 102, p. 82
APPENDIX, p. 126

BOTTOM: **lux-curva-ette**
lux, COLOR 115, p. 43
-curva, BLOCK 113, p. 70
-ette, QUILT 109, p. 114
APPENDIX, p. 138

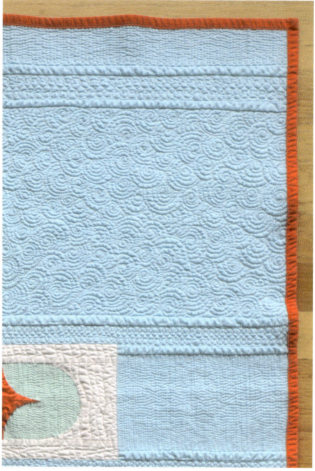

TOP LEFT: **nano-poly-ette**
nano, COLOR 112, p. 41
-ette, QUILT 109, p. 114
APPENDIX, p. 139

TOP RIGHT: **circum-poly-avore**
circum, COLOR 102, p. 36
-avore, QUILT 110, p. 118
APPENDIX, p. 140

BOTTOM: **lapis-curva-ism**
lapis, COLOR 114, p. 42
-ism, QUILT 108, p. 110
APPENDIX, p. 136

TOP: eco-parallel-esque
eco, COLOR 103, p. 37
-esque, QUILT 103, p. 86
APPENDIX, p. 128

BOTTOM: aqua-codex-athon
aqua, COLOR 104, p. 37
-athon, QUILT 107, p. 104
APPENDIX, p. 134

quilting gallery

TOP: **inter-proto-ism**
inter, COLOR 113, p. 42
-ism, QUILT 108, p. 110
APPENDIX, p. 137

BOTTOM: **paleo-domus-esque**
paleo, COLOR 111, p. 41
-esque, QUILT 103, p. 86
APPENDIX, p. 129

HOW TO: Half-Square Triangle

Half Square Triangle – 2"

Strips: Cut the specified number of 2⅞" x WOF strips from each fabric.

Squares: Cut the strips from the previous step into the specified number of 2⅞" x 2⅞" squares from each fabric.

Combos: Make the specified number of HST combinations from the pairs of squares (shown as Piece 1 and Piece 2).

a. Take one Piece 1 square and one Piece 2 square. Stack one on top of the other, right sides together. Draw a diagonal line with a water soluble fabric marker on the wrong side of the top square.

b. Sew a ¼" seam on either side of the line drawn in (a).

c. Cut along the center line. Press seams open. Trim triangle tails. You'll end up with two combined squares.

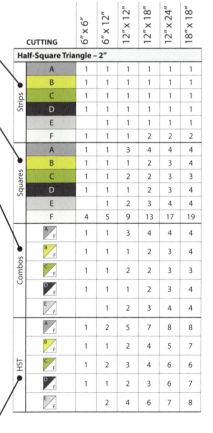

HST: How many HSTs will be used in the block. The combos sewn in the previous set will yield twice as many HSTs. In some patterns where an odd number of HSTs is called for, you will have one extra HST.

	CUTTING	6"x6"	6"x12"	12"x12"	12"x18"	12"x24"	18"x18"
Half-Square Triangle – 2"							
Strips	A	1	1	1	1	1	1
	B	1	1	1	1	1	1
	C	1	1	1	1	1	1
	D	1	1	1	1	1	1
	E		1	1	1	1	1
	F	1	1	1	2	2	2
Squares	A	1	1	3	4	4	4
	B	1	1	1	2	3	4
	C	1	1	2	2	3	3
	D	1	1	1	2	3	4
	E		1	2	3	4	4
	F	4	5	9	13	17	19
Combos	A/F	1	1	3	4	4	4
	B/F	1	1	1	2	3	4
	C/F	1	1	2	2	3	3
	D/F	1	1	1	2	3	4
	E/F		1	2	3	4	4
HST	A/F	1	2	5	7	8	8
	B/F	1	1	2	4	5	7
	C/F	1	2	3	4	6	6
	D/F	1	1	2	3	6	7
	E/F		2	4	6	7	8

Half Square Triangle – 3"

Follow the instructions for the 2" (finished) HST, substituting 3⅞" x WOF strips for 2⅞" x WOF and 3⅞" x 3⅞" squares for 2⅞" x 2⅞" squares.

HOW TO: Quarter Curve

Quarter Curve – 2"

Strips: Cut the given number of 2½" x WOF strips from each fabric.

Inner and Outer Curves: Trace and cut out the Inner and Outer Quarter Curve – 2" templates on p. 31. Cut the strips from the previous step into the specified number of Inner and Outer curve pieces using the templates.

Combos: Make the given number of Quarter Curve combinations.

a. Following the combinations in the chart, take one outer curve piece and one inner curve piece. Fold each in half and finger press a crease in each at the spot shown in the diagram.

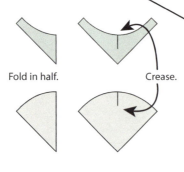

Fold in half.   Crease.

CUTTING		6" x 6"	6" x 12"	12" x 12"	12" x 18"	12" x 24"	18" x 18"
Quarter Curve – 2"							
Strips	A	1	1	1	1	2	2
	B	1	1	2	2	3	4
	C	1	1	1	1	2	3
†	A	2o	4o	12o	16o	24o	20o
	B	6i	8i	24i	32i	48i	64i
	C	4o	4o	12o	16o	24o	44o
Combos		2	4	12	16	24	20
		4	4	12	16	24	44

† Inner **(i)**/Outer **(o)** Curves

b. Place the two pieces right sides together with the outer piece on top. Align the center crease and pin.

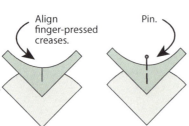

Align finger-pressed creases.   Pin.

c. Align the corners of the outer and inner curve pieces on the left side and pin. Repeat on the right side. Note: If you are unfamiliar with sewing curves, you may want to add more pins along the curve to hold the fabric in place while you sew. Keeping the outer curve piece on top, sew the curve with a ¼" seam.

d. Press the seam towards the outer curve, making sure not to stretch the edges. The block will measure 3½" square.

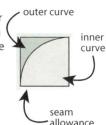

outer curve, inner curve, seam allowance

Quarter Curve – 3"

Follow the instructions for the 2" Quarter Curves, substituting 3½" x WOF strips for 2½" x WOF and 3" templates for 2" templates.

color, block & quilt

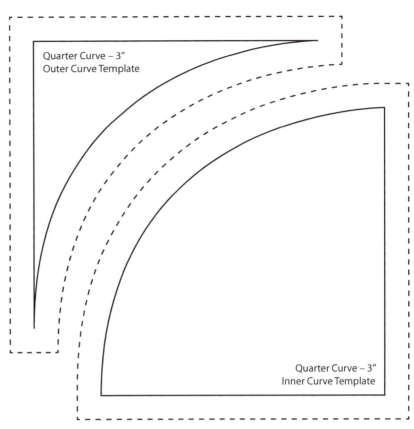

Quarter Curve – 3"
Outer Curve Template

Quarter Curve – 3"
Inner Curve Template

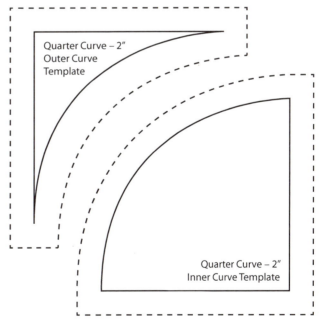

Quarter Curve – 2"
Outer Curve Template

Quarter Curve – 2"
Inner Curve Template

HOW TO: quarter curve

color

Color inspiration is all around us but is often ignored. Whether it's the scraps from chopping vegetables for dinner or the flowers blooming outside your front door, always keep a keen eye to even the smallest, insignificant parts of your day.

All of the color palettes, blocks and quilts are built on Robert Kaufman's Kona Cotton Solids. I've loved Kona Cotton since I began quilting, so they are always my go-to fabrics when making quilts from solids.

The Kona range has 243 colors (as of this writing). Each fabric in COLOR, BLOCK & QUILT is referenced by the Kona name and number (i.e. 'Ice Frappe-1173'). Use this information when shopping online or in person at your favorite quilt shop to make sure the right shade of color comes home with you!

These palettes aren't built upon schoolroom color theories but on my love of taking photographs of everything around me. I'm drawn to large, expansive landscapes and tight, closeup macro florals.

How do I go from an inspiration to a final palette?
When coming up with your own palettes, a photo is a great start, but don't let yourself be limited to exact reproductions of those tones. The palette can be built simply on the feelings the photo evoke — perhaps the calm of the sea or the fine details within a flower bud.

Start with a color that catches your eye — either visually or emotionally — and build from there. I cut up a Kona Cotton Solids color card (available at robertkaufman.com and quilt shops) into little color chips to help with this.

Let's use the picture above as our inspiration piece. It was taken while out on an expedition with my kids at a local rose garden. The first thing that catches my eye is the many shades of purple in the lavender flowers. I want at least three shades, but after going through all the purples, I end up with four.

Since I'm not looking for a monochromatic quilt this time around, I'll add some yellow and dark grey from the bee.

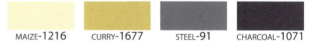

I'll finish out with a range of greens from the background.

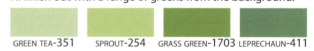

This leaves us with 12 colors, a couple more than the 6-8 colors in the palettes presented in this book. Plus, I seem to be unable to make a quilt without an almost-white color, so I'd still like to add that. My first instinct is to cut some of the greens and purples since I have four of each of them.

This is the final palette of eight. Maize ended up too similar to my almost-white Oyster. Tulip and Charcoal are both super dark, so I kept just Charcoal. Pansy was the final cut because there just wasn't enough contrast between it an the other purples and something had to go.

color, block & quilt

Green Tea and Leprechaun are the two greens I chose to keep because they looked the best with all the other colors. When building a palette, pick out all the colors and evaluate the entire palette together before finalizing your plans. Having the wrong shade of just one color can throw off the entire quilt.

I really like this grouping! Perhaps it will debut officially in COLOR, BLOCK & QUILT, VOLUME 2.

What do I do with the palette now?
Let's skip ahead a bit and say you've chosen your blocks and quilt. Now it's time to put your palette to use!

Take *-ruption* (QUILT 102, p. 82) as an example. It features nine blocks, each with a chunky border, on top of a background with a center column.

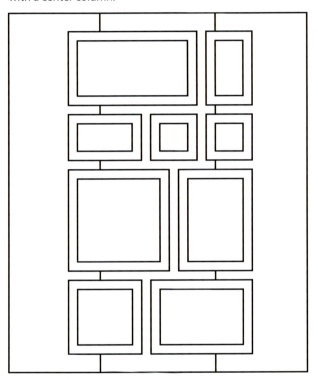

We'll say we want this quilt to be calm with a neutral background and the colors focused in the blocks (right, top illustration). A bold color should separate the blocks from the background in the chunky frame, so we'll use Steel, which is dark enough to make the blocks pop but light enough to stand out against the center column. The darkest neutral, Charcoal will be the center column color so it'll be bold enough to stand out while being mostly covered with blocks. Oyster will be the final color in the background, completing the calm look we were was going for.

We want blocks filled with color that pop against the neutral background (right, bottom illustration). We also want the background of the blocks to be the same Oyster as the background of the quilt to tie them together. The other colors from the palette are distributed through the blocks.

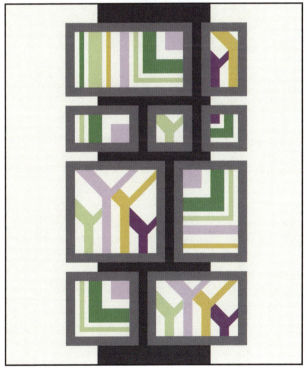

color assignments

QUILT 102
A: Oyster-1268
B: Steel-91
C: Charcoal-1071

BLOCK 105
A: Oyster-1268
B: Green Tea-351
C: Thistle-134
D: Curry-1677
E: Magenta-1214

BLOCK 106
A: Oyster-1268
B: Thistle-134
C: Leprechaun-411
D: Green Tea-351
E: Curry-1677

And now for something completely different.
Want to switch everything around and try something completely different? Let's say you're making a gift for you 4-year-old niece who just happens to love purple. This combination leaves out the Charcoal, which will be just perfect for the binding.

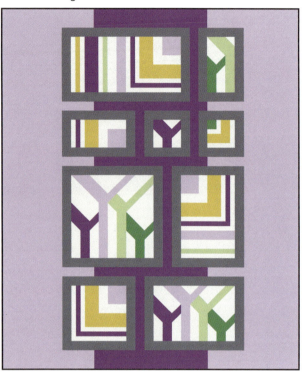

What about for the guys?
He wants lots of grey. She wants color! You get the idea.

color assignments

QUILT **102**
A: Thistle-134
B: Steel-91
C: Magenta-1214

BLOCK **105**
A: Oyster-1268
B: Magenta-1214
C: Thistle-134
D: Green Tea-351
E: Leprechaun-411

BLOCK **106**
A: Oyster-1268
B: Thistle-134
C: Curry-1677
D: Magenta-1214
E: Green Tea-351

color assignments

QUILT **102**
A: Charcoal-1071
B: Oyster-1268
C: Steel-91

BLOCK **105**
A: Charcoal-1071
B: Leprechaun-411
C: Steel-91
D: Green Tea-351
E: Curry-1677

BLOCK **106**
A: Charcoal-1071
B: Steel-91
C: Thistle-134
D: Leprechaun-411
E: Green Tea-351

The remainder of the COLOR section is filled with colors, fabrics and photographs. Sit back, enjoy and play with color.

COLOR:
contents

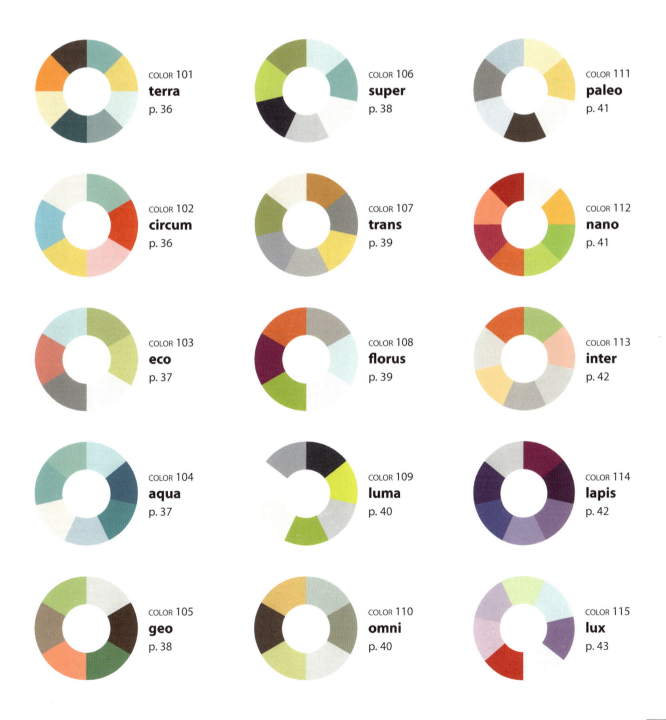

COLOR 101 **terra** p. 36

COLOR 102 **circum** p. 36

COLOR 103 **eco** p. 37

COLOR 104 **aqua** p. 37

COLOR 105 **geo** p. 38

COLOR 106 **super** p. 38

COLOR 107 **trans** p. 39

COLOR 108 **florus** p. 39

COLOR 109 **luma** p. 40

COLOR 110 **omni** p. 40

COLOR 111 **paleo** p. 41

COLOR 112 **nano** p. 41

COLOR 113 **inter** p. 42

COLOR 114 **lapis** p. 42

COLOR 115 **lux** p. 43

terra
COLOR 101

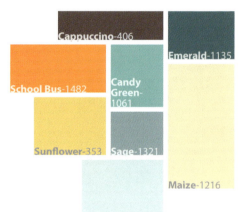

Cappuccino-406
Emerald-1135
School Bus-1482
Candy Green-1061
Sunflower-353
Sage-1321
Maize-1216
Ice Frappe-1173

circum
COLOR 102

Azure-1009
Ivory-1181
Pond-200
Corn Yellow-1089
Dusty Peach-1465
Tangerine-1370

36 color, block & quilt

eco
COLOR 103

Salmon-1483
Aqua-1005
Artichoke-347
White-1387
Zucchini-354
Mushroom-1239

Candy Green-1061
Pond-200
Aqua-1005
Caribbean-1064
Jade Green-1183
Dusty Blue-362
Bone-1037

aqua
COLOR 104

color

Sprout-254
Oyster-1268
Biscuit-1473
Chestnut-407

Leprechaun-411

Mango-192

geo
COLOR 105

super
COLOR 106

Cactus-199

Charcoal-1071

Olive-1263

Snow-1339

Ice Frappe-1173

Ash-1007

Candy Green-1061

38 color, block & quilt

trans
COLOR 107

Bone-1037
Corn Yellow-1089
Iron-408
Parchment-413
Amber-1479
Olive-1263
Mushroom-1239

Stone-1362
Peapod-414
Kumquat-410
Ice Frappe-1173
White-1387
Cerise-1066

florus
COLOR 108

luma
COLOR 109

White-1387
Charcoal-1071
Iron-408
Citrus-1077
Ash-1007
Peapod-414
Bone-1037

omni
COLOR 110

Cappuccino-406
Ochre-1704
Seafoam-1328
Sweet Pea-201
Oyster-1268
Zucchini-354

40 color, block & quilt

paleo
COLOR 111

Mushroom-1239 Maize-1216
Sunflower-353 Sky-1513
Cappuccino-406 Dusty Blue-362 Snow-1339

Poppy-1296 Kumquat-410 Cactus-199
Mango-192 White-1387 Pomegranate-1295
Chartreuse-1072 Papaya-149

nano
COLOR 112

color 41

inter
COLOR 113

- Oyster-1268
- Kumquat-410
- Sprout-254
- Peach-1281
- Putty-1303
- Parchment-413
- Cheddar-350

lapis
COLOR 114

- Tulip-327
- Ash-1007
- Cerise-1066
- Dark Violet-1485
- Lavender-1189
- Wisteria-1392
- Lapis-357

color, block & quilt

lux
COLOR 115

- Wisteria-1392
- White-1387
- Lipstick-1194
- Petunia-24
- Honey Dew-21
- Aqua-1005
- Thistle-134

color 43

block

Quilt blocks have been around nearly as long as quilts themselves; indeed, they are the building, ah, blocks of the vast majority of quilts, both traditional and modern. They're infinitely flexible, and serve as the basic unit of creativity both on their own and as part of an overall quilt design. There are an incredible wealth of block designs spanning hundreds of years of quilts, and they range from the painstakingly, minutely intricate down to the pure and simple. To me, the humble quilt block is the most iconic part of the entire tradition.

In this book, we extend blocks outside of their usual 12" x 12" comfort zone, bringing five additional block sizes into play. For some quilts, that variation itself can provide the backbone of a compelling quilt: a single block design repeated in a variety of sizes can result in an clean, modern look with enough visual pizazz to keep it interesting, in much the same way that a canon in classical music can form a fascinating and beautiful piece of music by repeating a simple melody with variations in timing, key, and so on. Examples of this type of quilt include *eco-parallel-esque* (p. 128) and *lapis-curva-ism* (p. 136).

Other quilts may use many blocks all with the same size, creating a sampler feel with a unifying theme drawn from the consistent shapes of the blocks; see *nano-poly-ette* (p. 139) and *trans-poly-asaurus* (p. 132) for examples. Dramatically varying both the blocks and sizes can create an almost dizzying array of visual ideas, taking the sampler quilt to a new level (for example, *circum-poly-avore*, p. 140).

If you aren't sure how a set of blocks will look when combined in the context of particular sizes within a quilt, I recommend using COLOR, BLOCK & QUILT: WORKBOOK (see *Resources*, p. 146) to help make sure you'll like the quilt you're composing before you commit it to fabric. Though sometimes the surprise of seeing the transformative effect of a new combination is half the fun!

BLOCK:
contents

BLOCK 101
-orbis
p. 46

BLOCK 106
-auto
p. 56

BLOCK 111
-insta
p. 66

BLOCK 102
-flora
p. 48

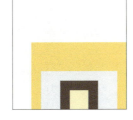
BLOCK 107
-domus
p. 58

BLOCK 112
-proto
p. 68

BLOCK 103
-rumpo
p. 50

BLOCK 108
-macro
p. 60

BLOCK 113
-curva
p. 70

BLOCK 104
-pluvia
p. 52

BLOCK 109
-tele
p. 62

BLOCK 114
-parallel
p. 72

BLOCK 105
-loco
p. 54

BLOCK 110
-retro
p. 64

BLOCK 115
-codex
p. 74

block

-orbis
BLOCK 101

Assembly

Instructions are written for the 12" x 12" ᶲ block. Assembly for all blocks is similar. Use these instructions along with the cutting chart and diagrams to make your sized block.

1. Cut fabric A as noted Cutting chart for your chosen block size.

2. Cut and assemble the quantity of **Quarter Curve – 2"** blocks listed in the Cutting chart to the right using the instructions on p. 30.

3. Assemble the quarter curves into half-circles. Press seams open.

4. Sew the groups into rows.

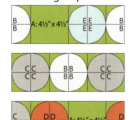

5. Sew the rows into the completed block.

CUTTING			6"x6"ᶲ	6"x12"ᶲ	12"x12"ᶲ	12"x18"ᶲ	12"x24"ᶲ	18"x18"ᶲ
	Dimensions	**Quantity**						
A	18½" x 1½"							2
	2½" x 2½"		1					
	2½" x 4½"						2	
	4½" x 4½"			1	2	3	2	4
	10½" x 4½"						1	
Quarter Curve – 2"								
Strips	A		1	1	2	3	4	4
	B			1	1	1	1	1
	C		1	1	1	1	1	2
	D		1	1	1	1	1	1
	E		1		1	1	1	1
Curves †	A		8o	14o	28o	42o	50o	56o
	B			4i	8i	12i	16i	16i
	C		4i	6i	10i	14i	14i	18i
	D		2i	4i	6i	8i	8i	10i
	E		2i		4i	8i	12i	12i
Combos	A/B			4	8	12	16	16
	A/C		4	6	10	14	14	18
	A/D		2	4	6	8	8	10
	A/E		2		4	8	12	12

ᶲ finished size
† Inner **(i)**/Outer **(o)** Curves

color, block & quilt

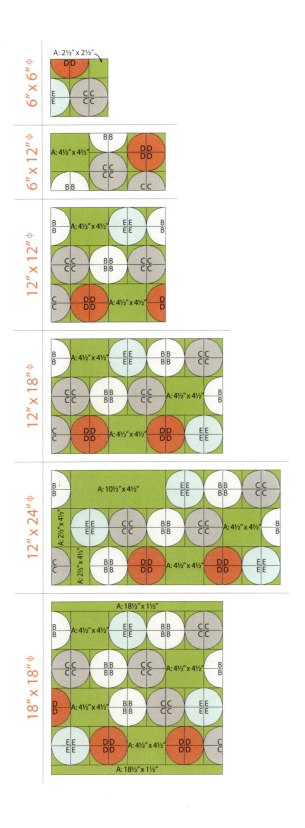

See this block in action: -athon, QUILT 107, p. 104 and p. 135

Colors used in block on both pages: florus, COLOR 108, p. 39

■ **A:** Peapod-414, □ **B:** White-1387, ▪ **C:** Stone-1362, ■ **D:** Kumquat-410, ▪ **E:** Ice Frappe-1173

-flora
BLOCK 102

Assembly

Instructions are written for the 12" x 18" ɸ block. Assembly for all blocks is similar. Use these instructions along with the cutting chart and diagrams to make your sized block.

1. Cut fabrics A and B as noted in the Cutting chart for your chosen block size.

2. Cut and assemble the quantity of **Quarter Curve – 2"** blocks listed in the Cutting chart to the right using the instructions on p. 30.

   Cut and assemble the quantity of **Half-Square Triangle – 2"** blocks listed in the Cutting chart to the right using the instructions on p. 29.

3. Assemble each group, half- and full-circles. Press seams open.

   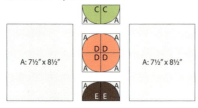

4. Sew together the center column and flower base.

   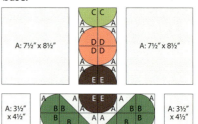

5. Sew the top and bottom portions into rows. Sew the two rows together into the completed block.

   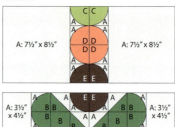

CUTTING			6"×6" ϕ	6"×12" ϕ	12"×12" ϕ	12"×18" ϕ	12"×24" ϕ	18"×18" ϕ
	Dimensions	**Quantity**						
A	2½" × 2½"	1						
	18½" × 2½"							1
	3½" × 4½"						2	2
	4½" × 4½"				1		1	
	2½" × 8½"	1		1				
	4½" × 8½"				2		2	
	7½" × 8½"					2		
	8½" × 8½"						1	
	7½" × 12½"							2
B	2½" × 2½"		1	1	2	2	4	2

Quarter Curve – 2"

		6"×6"	6"×12"	12"×12"	12"×18"	12"×24"	18"×18"
Strips	A	1	1	1	1	2	2
	B		1	1	1	1	1
	C			1	1	1	1
	D		1	1	1	1	1
	E	1	1	1	1	1	1
Curves †	A	4o	10o	10o	14o	24o	18o
	B			4i	4i	8i	6i
	C		2i		2i	2i	4i
	D		4i	2i	4i	6i	4i
	E	4i	4i	4i	4i	8i	4i
Combos	A/B			4	4	8	6
	A/C			2		2	2	4
	A/D		4	2	4	6	4
	A/E	4	4	4	4	8	4

Half-Square Triangle – 2"

		6"×6"	6"×12"	12"×12"	12"×18"	12"×24"	18"×18"
Strips	A	1	1	1	1	1	1
	B	1	1	1	1	1	1
Squares	A	2	2	2	2	4	2
	B	2	2	2	2	4	2
HST Combos	A/B	2	2	2	2	4	2
HST	A/B	3	3	4	4	8	4

ϕ finished size
† Inner (**i**)/Outer (**o**) Curves

See this block in action: -mania, QUILT 104, p. 92 and p. 130
-avore, QUILT 110, p. 118 and p. 140
Colors used in block: geo, COLOR 105, p. 38
A: Oyster-1268, **B:** Leprechaun-411, **C:** Sprout-254,
D: Mango-192, **E:** Chestnut-407

BLOCK 102: -flora   49

-rumpo
BLOCK 103

Assembly

Instructions are written for the 12" x 12" ⌽ block. Assembly for all blocks is similar. Use these instructions along with the cutting chart and diagrams to make your sized block.

1. Cut fabrics A, C and D as noted in the Cutting chart for your chosen block size.

2. Cut and assemble the quantity of **Quarter Curve – 2"** blocks listed in the Cutting chart to the right using the instructions on p. 30.

3. Assemble the rows of quarter curves and squares. Press seams open.

   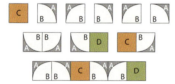

4. Sew the rows together, nesting seams. Press seams open to reduce bulk.

   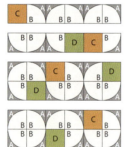

Note: Some blocks have strips to the left/right and top/bottom. Refer to the assembly diagram for each block.

CUTTING			6"x6"⌽	6"x12"⌽	12"x12"⌽	12"x18"⌽	12"x24"⌽	18"x18"⌽
	Dimensions	**Quantity**						
A	4½" x 1½"	2						
	6½" x 1½"	2						
	12½" x 1½"				2	2		
	16½" x 1½"							2
	18½" x 1½"							2
C	2½" x 2½"			1	4	6	8	8
D	2½" x 2½"		1	1	4	5	8	7
Quarter Curve – 2"								
Strips	A		1	1	2	3	4	4
	B		1	1	2	3	4	4
†	A		3o	10o	28o	37o	56o	49o
	B		3i	10i	28i	37i	56i	49i
‡			3	10	28	37	56	49

⌽ finished size
† Inner (**i**)/Outer (**o**) Curves
‡ Combos

See this BLOCK in action: -asaurus, QUILT 105, p. 96 and p. 132

Colors used in BLOCK: trans, COLOR 107, p. 39
■ **A:** Mushroom-1239, ☐ **B:** Bone-1037, ■ **C:** Amber-1479,
■ **D:** Olive-1263

color, block & quilt

BLOCK 103: rumpo 51

-pluvia
BLOCK 104

Assembly

Instructions are written for the 12" x 12" ᶲ block. Assembly for all blocks is similar. Use these instructions along with the cutting chart and diagrams to make your sized block.

1. Cut fabrics A, B, C, and D as noted in the Cutting chart for your chosen block size.

2. Cut and assemble the quantity of **Quarter Curve – 2"** blocks listed in the Cutting chart to the right using the instructions on p. 30.

   Cut and assemble the quantity of **Half-Square Triangle – 2"** blocks listed in the Cutting chart on the opposite page using the instructions on p. 29.

3. Assemble the rows of quarter curves, HSTs and squares/rectangles. Press seams open.

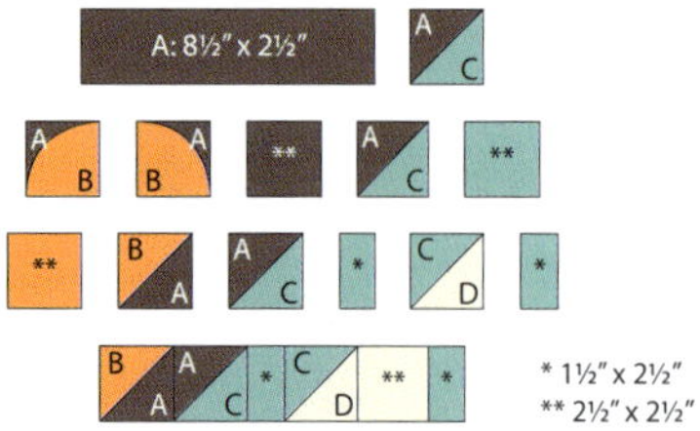

   * 1½" x 2½"
   ** 2½" x 2½"

4. Sew the rows together. Press seams open to reduce bulk. Finish by sewing the two A: 12½" x 1½" piece to the left and right sides. Press towards the outside.

Note: *While some blocks have strips on the top/bottom and/or left/right, not all do. Refer to the diagram for each block.*

CUTTING		6" x 6" ᶲ	6" x 12" ᶲ	12" x 12" ᶲ	12" x 18" ᶲ	12" x 24" ᶲ	18" x 18" ᶲ
	Dimensions	**Quantity**					
A	6½" x 1½"	2					
A	12½" x 1½"			2			
A	2½" x 2½"	1	2	3	2	2	2
A	4½" x 2½"				2	2	2
A	8½" x 2½"			1			
A	12½" x 2½"				2		2
A	18½" x 3½"						2
A	12½" x 5½"					2	
B	1½" x 2½"				5	5	5
B	2½" x 2½"	1		1	1	1	1
B	3½" x 2½"				1	1	1
B	4½" x 2½"				1	1	1
C	1½" x 2½"		6	5	5	5	5
C	2½" x 2½"		1	1	1	1	1
C	3½" x 2½"			1	1	1	1
C	4½" x 2½"			1	1	1	1
D	2½" x 2½"		1	1	2	2	2
Quarter Curve – 2"							
Strips	A	1	1	1	1	1	1
Strips	B	1		1	1	1	1
Strips	C		1	1	1	1	1
Strips	D		1	1	1	1	1
Curves †	A	2o	1o	4o	4o	4o	4o
Curves †	B	2i		2i	2i, 2o	2i, 2o	2i, 2o
Curves †	C		1i, 2o	2i, 2o	2i, 2o	2i, 2o	2i, 2o
Curves †	D		2i	2i	4i	4i	4i
Combos	A/B	2		2	2	2	2
Combos	A/C		1	2	2	2	2
Combos	B/D				2	2	2
Combos	C/D		2	2	2	2	2

ᶲ finished size † Inner (i)/Outer (o) Curves

Half-Square Triangle – 2"		6"×6" ⌀	6"×12" ⌀	12"×12" ⌀	12"×18" ⌀	12"×24" ⌀	18"×18" ⌀
Strips	A	1	1	1	1	1	1
	B	1	1	1	1	1	1
	C			1	1	1	1
	D		1	1	1	1	1
Squares	A	1	3	3	4	4	4
	B	1	1	1	3	3	3
	C		3	3	3	3	3
	D		1	1	2	2	2
Combos	A/B	1	1	1	2	2	2
	A/C		2	2	2	2	2
	B/D				1	1	1
	C/D		1	1	1	1	1
HST	A/B	2	1	2	4	4	4
	A/C		3	4	4	4	4
	B/D					2	2	2
	C/D			2	2	2	2	2

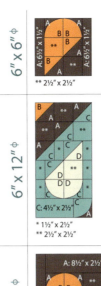

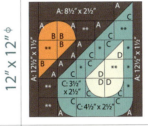

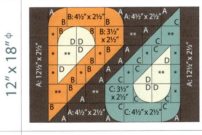

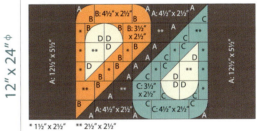

See this block in action:
-asaurus, QUILT 105, p. 96 and p. 132
-scope, QUILT 106, p. 100 and p. 125

Colors used in block on opposite page and illustrations: terra, COLOR 101, p. 36
A: Cappuccino-406, **B:** School Bus-1482, **C:** Candy Green-1061, **D:** Maize-1216

Colors used in block on this page: trans, COLOR 107, p. 39
A: Mushroom-1239, **B:** Amber-1479, **C:** Olive-1263, **D:** Bone-1037

BLOCK 104: -pluvia

-loco
BLOCK 105

Assembly

Instructions show the 12" x 12" ᶲ block. Assembly for all blocks is similar. Use these instructions along with the cutting chart and diagrams to make your sized block.

1. Cut fabrics A-E as noted in the Cutting chart for your chosen block size.

2. Cut and assemble the quantity of **Half-Square Triangle – 2"** blocks listed in the Cutting chart on the opposite page using the instructions on p. 29.

3. Sew each row of squares, rectangles and HSTs. *When no dimensions are specified in the diagram, use a 2½" x 2½" piece. Press seams open.*

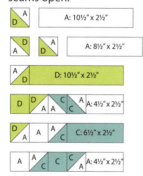

4. Sew the rows together, nesting seams. Press entire block.

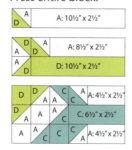

5. These blocks are assembled sideways. The completed blocks should be rotated 90 degrees to the right.

CUTTING		6" x 6" ᶲ	6" x 12" ᶲ	12" x 12" ᶲ	12" x 18" ᶲ	12" x 24" ᶲ	18" x 18" ᶲ
	Dimensions	**Quantity**					
A	2½" x 2½"	2	1	2	7	6	5
	4½" x 2½"		1	2	2	5	5
	6½" x 2½"				1	2	3
	8½" x 2½"			1			
	10½" x 2½"			1			1
B	2½" x 2½"	1			1	2	1
	4½" x 2½"	1					
	6½" x 2½"				1	2	
	8½" x 2½"						1
C	2½" x 2½"			1	1	1	2
	6½" x 2½"			1			
	10½" x 2½"				1	1	
	14½" x 2½"						1
D	2½" x 2½"		1	1			
	8½" x 2½"				1	1	
	10½" x 2½"		1	1			
	12½" x 2½"						1
E	2½" x 2½"				1		1
	4½" x 2½"				1	1	
	6½" x 2½"			1			1

ᶲ finished size

Half-Square Triangle – 2"

		6"x6"	6"x12"	12"x12"	12"x18"	12"x24"	18"x18"
Strips	A	1	1	1	1	1	1
	B	1			1	1	1
	C			1	1	1	1
	D		1	1	1	1	1
	E		1		1	1	1
Squares	A	2	4	6	13	14	15
	B	2			3	8	3
	C			3	4	4	6
	D		2	3	5	5	5
	E		2		3	3	3
Combos	A/B	2			3	6	3
	A/C			3	3	3	5
	A/D		2	3	4	3	4
	A/E		2		3	2	3
	D/C				1	1	1
	B/D					1	
	B/E					1	
HST	A/B	4			5	12	5
	A/C			5	5	5	9
	A/D			3	6	7	6	8
	A/E			3		5	4	5
	D/C				1	1	1
	B/D					1	
	B/E					1	

See this BLOCK in action: -ruption, QUILT 102, p. 82 and p. 126

Colors used in BLOCK: super, COLOR 106, p. 38
A: Snow-1339, B: Olive-1263, C: Candy Green-1061,
D: Cactus-199, E: Ice Frappe-1173

BLOCK 105: -loco

-auto
BLOCK 106

Assembly

Instructions are written for the 12" x 18" ᶲ block. Assembly for all blocks is similar. Use these instructions along with the cutting chart and diagrams to make your sized block.

1. Cut fabrics A-E as noted in the Cutting chart for your chosen block size.

2. Sew one A: 4½" x 2½" to the left side of the B: 4½" x 4½" piece. Press seam to the outside.

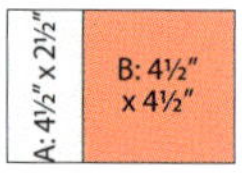

3. Sew one A: 6½" x 2½" to the bottom of the unit from the previous step. Press.

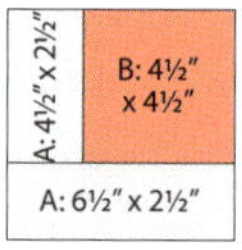

4. Sew one C: 6½" x 3½" to the left side of the unit from the previous step. Press.

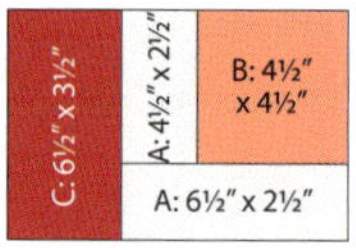

5. Continue, sewing pieces to the bottom and left, pressing after each piece.

CUTTING	Dimensions	Quantity	6" x 6" ᶲ	6" x 12" ᶲ	12" x 12" ᶲ	12" x 18" ᶲ	12" x 24" ᶲ	18" x 18" ᶲ
A	2½" x 1½"	1						
A	3½" x 1½"	1						
A	5½" x 1½"	1						
A	6½" x 1½"	1	2					
A	9½" x 1½"				1	1	1	1
A	10½" x 1½"				1	1	1	1
A	11½" x 1½"				1	1	1	1
A	12½" x 1½"				1	2	4	1
A	17½" x 1½"							1
A	18½" x 1½"							1
A	4½" x 2½"			1	1	1	1	1
A	6½" x 2½"			1	1	1	1	1
A	12½" x 2½"					1	1	
A	14½" x 2½"							1
A	16½" x 2½"							1
B	2½" x 2½"	1						
B	12½" x 2½"					1	1	1
B	14½" x 2½"							1
B	4½" x 4½"			1	1	1	1	1
C	12½" x 1½"						1	
C	3½" x 2½"	1						
C	5½" x 2½"	1						
C	6½" x 3½"			1	1	1	1	1
C	9½" x 3½"				1	1	1	1
D	6½" x 1½"				1			
D	10½" x 1½"				1	1	1	1
D	11½" x 1½"				1	1	1	1
D	12½" x 3½"						1	
E	12½" x 1½"					1	1	
E	16½" x 1½"							1
E	17½" x 1½"							1

ᶲ finished size

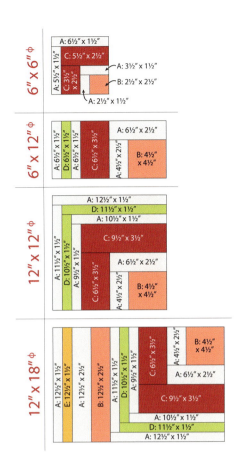
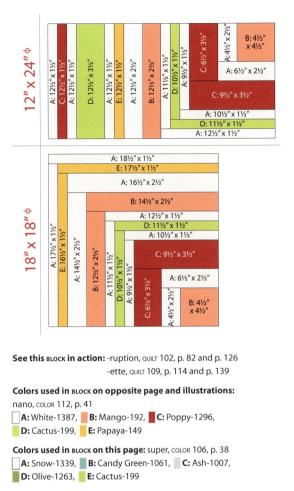

See this block in action: -ruption, QUILT 102, p. 82 and p. 126
 -ette, QUILT 109, p. 114 and p. 139

Colors used in block on opposite page and illustrations:
nano, COLOR 112, p. 41
 A: White-1387, **B:** Mango-192, **C:** Poppy-1296,
 D: Cactus-199, **E:** Papaya-149

Colors used in block on this page: super, COLOR 106, p. 38
 A: Snow-1339, **B:** Candy Green-1061, **C:** Ash-1007,
 D: Olive-1263, **E:** Cactus-199

BLOCK 106: -auto

-domus
BLOCK 107

Assembly

Instructions are written for the 12" x 18" ᵠ block. Assembly for all blocks is similar. Use these instructions along with the cutting chart and diagrams to make your sized block.

1. Cut fabrics A-F as noted in the Cutting chart for your chosen block size.

2. Sew two E: 2½" x 1½" to either side of the F: 2½" x 2½" piece. Press seams towards E.

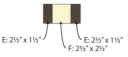

3. Sew one E: 4½" x 1½" to the top of the unit from the previous step. Press seams towards E.

4. Sew two D: 3½" x 2½" to either side of the unit from the previous step. Press seams towards D.

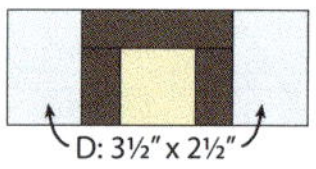

5. Continue, sewing pieces to the top and left/right, pressing towards the outside after each piece.

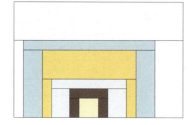

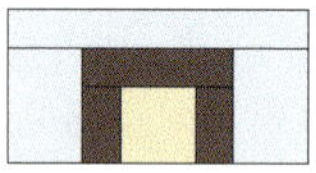

CUTTING	Dimensions	6" x 6" ᵠ	6" x 12" ᵠ	12" x 12" ᵠ	12" x 18" ᵠ	12" x 24" ᵠ	18" x 18" ᵠ
		Quantity					
A	8½" x 1½"				1	1	1
	6½" x 2½"	1					
	7½" x 2½"			1			
	6½" x 3½"		1				
	8½" x 3½"				1		1
	18½" x 4½"				1		
	24½" x 4½"					1	
	12½" x 5½"			1			
	9½" x 8½"					1	
	18½" x 10½"						1
B	14½" x 1½"				1	1	1
	7½" x 2½"				2	2	2
C	4½" x 1½"	1	1	2	2	2	2
	4½" x 2½"	1					
	9½" x 2½"		1				
	10½" x 3½"			1	1	1	1
D	3½" x 1½"	1					
	8½" x 1½"		1	1	1	1	1
	3½" x 2½"	1	2	2	2	2	2
E	2½" x 1½"		2	2	2	2	2
	3½" x 1½"	1					
	4½" x 1½"		1	1	1	1	1
F	2½" x 2½"		1	1	1	1	1

ᵠ finished size

See this BLOCK in action: -esque, QUILT 103, p. 86 and p. 129
-ette, QUILT 109, p. 114 and p. 139

Colors used in BLOCK: paleo, COLOR 111, p. 41

☐ **A:** Snow-1339, ■ **B:** Dusty Blue-362, ■ **C:** Sunflower-353,
■ **D:** Sky-1513, ■ **E:** Cappuccino-406, ■ **F:** Maize-1216

color, block & quilt

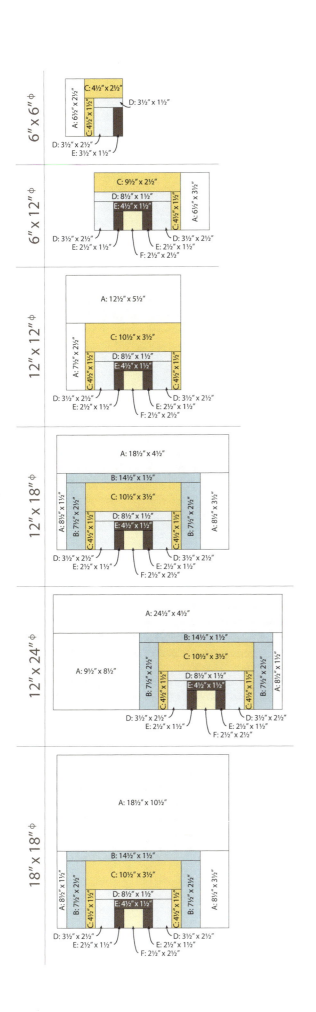

BLOCK 107: domus

-macro
BLOCK 108

Assembly

Instructions are written for the 12" x 12"⌀ block. Assembly for all blocks is similar. Use these instructions along with the cutting chart and diagrams to make your sized block.

1. Cut fabrics B, C, and E as noted in the Cutting chart for your chosen block size.

2. Cut and assemble the quantity of **Quarter Curve – 2"** blocks listed in the Cutting chart to the right using the instructions on p. 30.

3. Assemble the rows of quarter curves and squares. Press seams open.

4. Sew the rows together. Press seams open.

   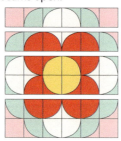

Note: Some blocks have strips on the top/bottom and/or left/right. Refer to the diagram for each block for strip placement.

CUTTING			6" x 6"⌀	6" x 12"⌀	12" x 12"⌀	12" x 18"⌀	12" x 24"⌀	18" x 18"⌀
	Dimensions	**Quantity**						
B	12½" x 1½"					2		
	16½" x 1½"							2
	18½" x 1½"							2
	2½" x 2½"						4	4
	4½" x 2½"							4
C	2½" x 2½"						4	
	4½" x 2½"						4	
E	2½" x 2½"		1	1	4			
Quarter Curve – 2"								
Strips	A		1	1	1	1	1	1
	B		1	1	1	2	3	2
	C		1	1	1	1	2	1
	D		1	1	2	2	2	2
	E		1	1	1	2	2	2
Inner(i)/Outer(o) Curves	A		1i	4i	4i	4i	4i	4i
	B		1o, 3i	4o, 8i	4o, 12i	12o, 12i	16o, 24i	16o, 12i
	C		2o, 2i	6o, 2i	8o, 8i	8o, 8i	20o, 8i	8o, 8i
	D		3o, 2i	4o, 3i	12o, 8i	12o, 12i	12o, 12i	12o, 16i
	E		2o	3o	8o	12o, 8i	12o, 12i	16o, 12i
Combos	B/A		1	4	4	4	4	4
	B/E					8	12	12
	C/B		2	6	8	8	20	8
	D/B		1	2	4	4	4	4
	D/C		2	2	8	8	8	8
	E/D		2	3	8	12	12	16

⌀ finished size

color, block & quilt

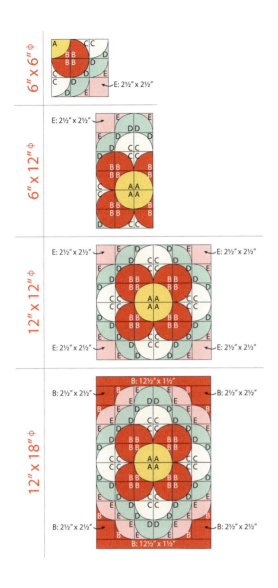
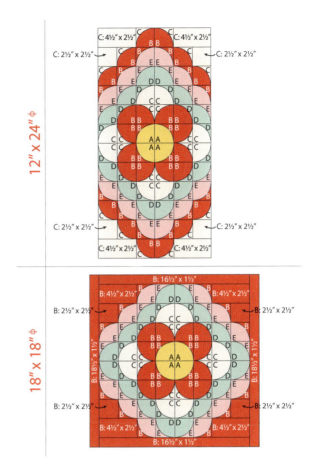

See this BLOCK in action: -mania, QUILT 104, p. 92 and p. 130
-avore, QUILT 110, p. 118 and p. 140

Colors used in BLOCK on opposite page and illustrations:
circum, COLOR 102, p. 36
A: Corn Yellow-1089, **B:** Tangerine-1370, **C:** Ivory-1181,
D: Pond-200, **E:** Dusty Peach-1465

Colors used in BLOCK on this page: geo, COLOR 105, p. 38
A: Sprout-254, **B:** Oyster-1268, **C:** Mango-192,
D: Leprechaun-411, **E:** Chestnut-407

BLOCK 108: -macro

-tele
BLOCK 109

Assembly

Instructions show the 12" x 12"ᶲ block. Assembly for all blocks is similar. Use these instructions along with the cutting chart and diagrams to make your sized block.

1. Cut and assemble the quantity of **Half-Square Triangle – 3"** blocks listed in the Cutting chart to the right using the instructions on p. 29.

2. Sew each row of HSTs making sure the orientation of each HST matches the diagram. Press seams open.

3. Sew the rows together. Press seams open.

CUTTING		6"x6"ᶲ	6"x12"ᶲ	12"x12"ᶲ	12"x18"ᶲ	12"x24"ᶲ	18"x18"ᶲ
Half-Square Triangle – 3"							
Strips	A	1	1	1	1	1	1
	B	1	1	1	1	1	1
	C	1	1	1	1	1	1
	D	1	1	1	1	1	1
	E		1	1	1	1	1
	F	1	1	1	2	2	2
Squares	A	1	1	3	4	4	4
	B	1	1	1	2	3	4
	C	1	1	2	2	3	3
	D	1	1	1	2	3	4
	E		1	2	3	4	4
	F	4	5	9	13	17	19
Combos	A/F	1	1	3	4	4	4
	B/F	1	1	1	2	3	4
	C/F	1	1	2	2	3	3
	D/F	1	1	1	2	3	4
	E/F		1	2	3	4	4
HST	A/F	1	2	5	7	8	8
	B/F	1	1	2	4	5	7
	C/F	1	2	3	4	6	6
	D/F	1	1	2	3	6	7
	E/F		2	4	6	7	8

ᶲ finished size

color, block & quilt

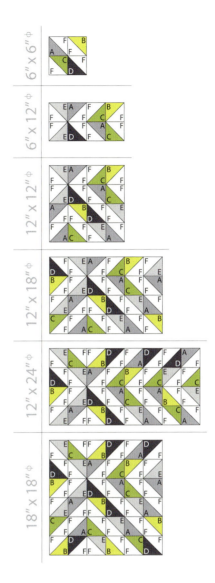

See this block in action: -asaurus, QUILT 105, p. 96, p. 131 and p. 132
-ette, QUILT 109, p. 114 and p. 139

Colors used in BLOCK: luma, COLOR 109, p. 40
- **A:** Iron-408, **B:** Citrus-1077, **C:** Peapod-414,
- **D:** Charcoal-1071, **E:** Ash-1007, **F:** White-1387

BLOCK 109: -tele **63**

-retro
BLOCK 110

Assembly

Instructions are written for the 12" x 12" ⌀ block. Assembly for all blocks is similar. Use these instructions along with the cutting chart and diagrams to make your sized block.

1. Cut fabric A as noted in the Cutting chart for your chosen block size.

2. Cut and assemble the quantity of **Quarter Curve – 2"** blocks listed in the Cutting chart to the right using the instructions on p. 30.

3. Assemble the rows of quarter curves. Pressing seams in opposite directions.

   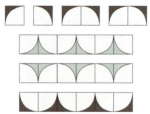

4. Sew the rows together. Press seams open to reduce bulk.

   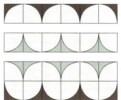

5. Sew the two A: 12½" x 2½" pieces to the top and bottom. Press towards A.

   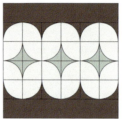

Note: *Each block has different strips used in Step 5 and some have strips sewn on the sides as well. Refer to the diagram for each block for strip placement.*

CUTTING		6"x 6"⌀	6"x 12"⌀	12"x 12"⌀	12"x 18"⌀	12"x 24"⌀	18"x 18"⌀
	Dimensions	**Quantity**					
A	6½" x 1½"	2					
	12½" x 1½"		2		2		
	16½" x 1½"						2
	18½" x 1½"						2
	4½" x 2½"			2			
	12½" x 2½"			2			
	16½" x 2½"					2	
	24½" x 2½"					2	
Quarter Curve – 2"							
Strips	A	1	1	1	1	2	2
	B	1	1	2	2	3	4
	C	1	1	1	1	2	3
†	A	20o	40o	120o	160o	240o	200o
	B	6i	8i	24i	32i	48i	64i
	C	4o	4o	12o	16o	24o	44o
Combos	A/B	2	4	12	16	24	20
	C/B	4	4	12	16	24	44

⌀ finished size
† Inner **(i)**/Outer **(o)** Curves

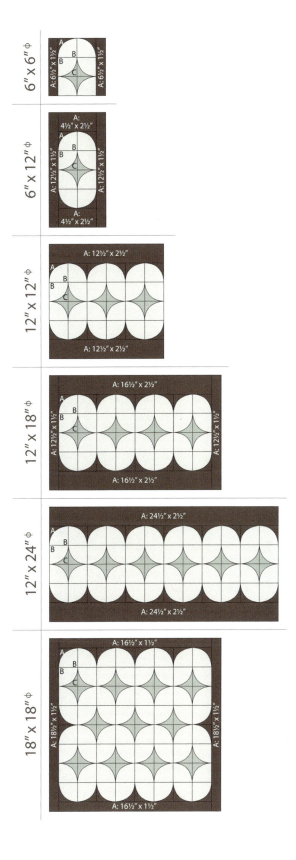

See this block in action: -cosm, QUILT 101, p. 78 and p. 124
-avore, QUILT 110, p. 118 and p. 140

Colors used in block: omni, COLOR 110, p. 40
■ A: Cappuccino-406, ☐ B: Oyster-1268, ☐ C: Seafoam-1328

BLOCK 110: -retro   65

-insta
BLOCK 111

Assembly

Instructions show the 12" x 18" ᶲ block. Assembly for all blocks is similar. Use these instructions along with the cutting chart and diagrams to make your sized block.

1. Cut fabrics A-E as noted in the Cutting chart for your chosen block size.

2. Sew the D: 4½" x 4½" and C: 4½" x 4½" to either side of the B: 4½" x 1½" piece. Press towards B.

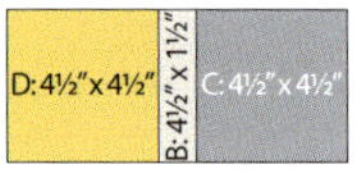

3. Sew two B: 9½" x 1½" pieces to the top and bottom. Press towards B.

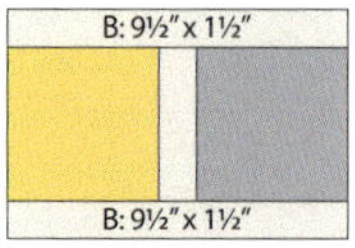

4. Sew B: 6½" x 2½" piece to the right side. Press towards B. Sew B: 7½" x 6½" piece to the left side. Press towards B.

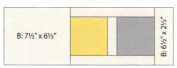

5. Sew two A: 18½" x 3½" pieces to the top and bottom. Press towards B.

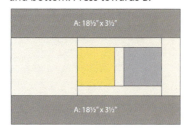

	CUTTING		6" x 6" ᶲ	6" x 12" ᶲ	12" x 12" ᶲ	12" x 18" ᶲ	12" x 24" ᶲ	18" x 18" ᶲ
	Dimensions	**Quantity**						
A	6½" x 2½"		1					
	6½" x 3½"			2				
	12½" x 3½"				2			
	18½" x 3½"					2		
	24½" x 3½"						2	
	18½" x 6½"							2
B	3½" x 1½"		2					
	4½" x 1½"			2	2	1	2	1
	6½" x 1½"		1					
	9½" x 1½"						2	2
	14½" x 1½"						2	
	6½" x 2½"			1	1	1	1	1
	6½" x 6½"				1			
	7½" x 6½"					1		1
	8½" x 6½"						1	
C	4½" x 3½"		1					
	4½" x 4½"				1	1	1	1
D	4½" x 4½"			1		1	1	1
E	4½" x 4½"						1	

ᶲ finished size

See this BLOCK in action: -asaurus, QUILT 105, p. 96 and p. 132
-ette, QUILT 109, p. 114 and p. 139

Colors used in BLOCK: trans, COLOR 107, p. 39
■ **A:** Mushroom-1239, ☐ **B:** Bone-1037, ■ **C:** Iron-408,
■ **D:** Corn Yellow-1089, ■ **E:** Olive-1263

color, block & quilt

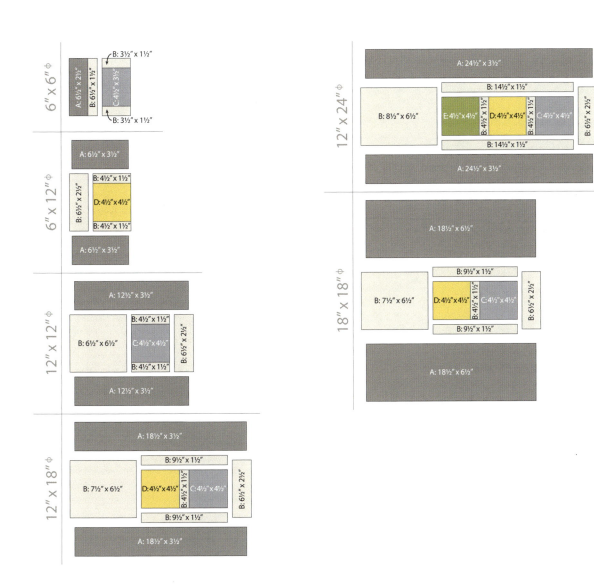

BLOCK 111: insta

-proto
BLOCK 112

Assembly

Instructions show the 12" x 12" ⌀ block. Assembly for all blocks is similar. Use these instructions along with the cutting chart and diagrams to make your sized block.

1. Cut fabrics A-D as noted in the Cutting chart for your chosen block size.

2. Assemble each row of pieces.

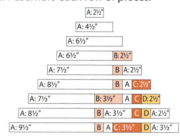

3. Sew the rows together, nesting seams at the intersections. Make sure to center the strip to the unit above. Press seams to one side.

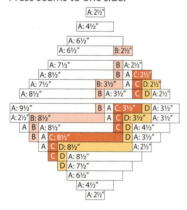

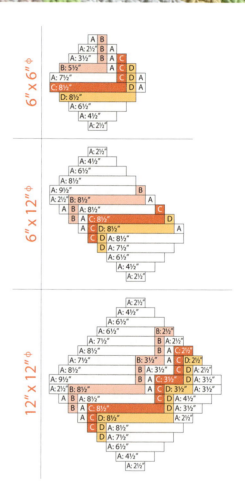

4. Trim to 12½" x 12½". *Note: After trimming, the bias-cut edge can easily stretch. Handle carefully and starch to help prevent stretching.*

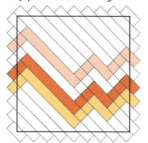

68   color, block & quilt

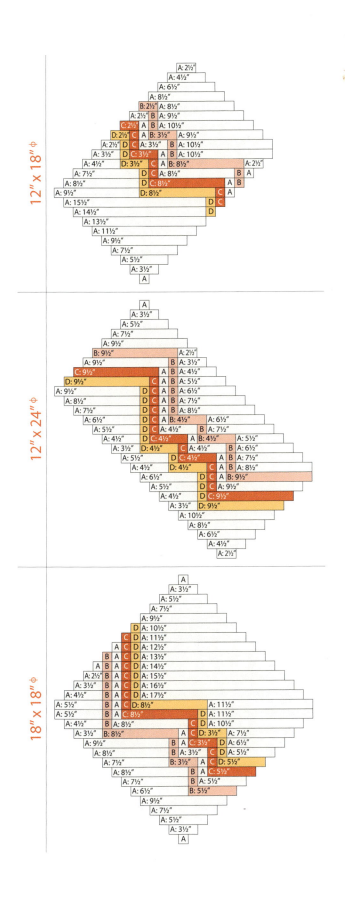

	CUTTING	6" x 6" ϕ	6" x 12" ϕ	12" x 12" ϕ	12" x 18" ϕ	12" x 24" ϕ	18" x 18" ϕ
	Dimensions	**Quantity**					
A	1½" x 1½"	6	5	7	8	11	15
	2½" x 1½"	2	3	6	4	2	1
	3½" x 1½"	1		4	3	4	5
	4½" x 1½"	1	2	3	2	7	2
	5½" x 1½"				1	6	6
	6½" x 1½"	1	2	3	1	6	2
	7½" x 1½"	1	1	3	2	5	5
	8½" x 1½"		3	4	4	4	3
	9½" x 1½"		1	1	4	4	3
	10½" x 1½"				3	1	2
	11½" x 1½"				1		3
	12½" x 1½"						1
	13½" x 1½"				1		1
	14½" x 1½"				1		1
	15½" x 1½"				1		1
	16½" x 1½"						1
	17½" x 1½"						1
B	1½" x 1½"	3	3	6	6	10	12
	2½" x 1½"			1	1		
	3½" x 1½"			1	1		1
	4½" x 1½"					2	
	5½" x 1½"	1					1
	8½" x 1½"		1	1	1		1
	9½" x 1½"					2	
C	1½" x 1½"	3	3	6	6	10	12
	2½" x 1½"			1	1		
	3½" x 1½"			1	1		1
	4½" x 1½"					2	
	5½" x 1½"						1
	8½" x 1½"	1	1	1	1		1
	9½" x 1½"					2	
D	1½" x 1½"	3	3	6	6	10	12
	2½" x 1½"			1	1		
	3½" x 1½"			1	1		1
	4½" x 1½"					2	
	5½" x 1½"						1
	8½" x 1½"	1	1	1	1		1
	9½" x 1½"					2	

ϕ finished size

See this BLOCK in action: -ism, QUILT 108, p. 110 and p. 137

Colors used in BLOCK: inter, COLOR 113, p. 42

A: Oyster-1268, **B:** Peach-1281, **C:** Kumquat-410, **D:** Cheddar-350

BLOCK 112: -proto

-curva
BLOCK 113

Assembly

Instructions are written for the 12" x 18" ⌽ block. Assembly for all blocks is similar. Use these instructions along with the cutting chart and diagrams to make your sized block.

1. Cut fabrics B, C and D as noted in the Cutting chart for your chosen block size.

2. Cut and assemble the quantity of **Quarter Curve – 3"** blocks listed in the Cutting chart to the right using the instructions on p. 30.

3. Assemble the rows of quarter curves and rectangles. Press seams open.

4. Sew the rows together. Press seams open.

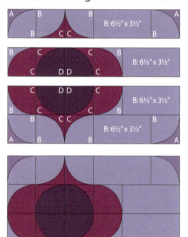

See this block in action: -ism, QUILT 108, p. 110 and p. 136
-ette, QUILT 109, p. 114 and p. 138

Colors used in block, top: lux, COLOR 115, p. 43
A: Lipstick-1194, **C:** Thistle-134, **D:** Honey Dew-21, **E:** Wisteria-1392

Colors used in block, bottom and illustrations: lapis, COLOR 114, p. 42
A: Wisteria-1392, **B:** Lavender-1189, **C:** Cerise-1066, **D:** Dark Violet-1485, **E:** Ash-1007, **F:** Tulip-327

color, block & quilt

CUTTING

	Dimensions	Quantity	6"x6" ⌀	6"x12" ⌀	12"x12" ⌀	12"x18" ⌀	12"x24" ⌀	18"x18" ⌀
B	6½" x 3½"					4		
C	3½" x 3½"						4	
C	9½" x 3½"						4	
D	3½" x 3½"							4
D	6½" x 3½"							2
D	9½" x 3½"							2

Quarter Curve – 3"

		6"x6"	6"x12"	12"x12"	12"x18"	12"x24"	18"x18"
Strips	A	1	1	1	1	2	1
	B		1	1	2		2
	C	1			2	1	1
	D	1	1		1	2	2
	E	1	1	2			
	F			2			
Inner(i)/Outer(o) Curves	A	1o, 2i	2i	4o	4o	8o, 4i	8i
	B		2o, 4i	4i	4o, 8i	4i	12o, 8i
	C	2o, 1i			8o, 4i	4o, 8i	4o
	D	1o	4o, 2i		4i	4o	6o, 6i
	E	1i	2o	4o, 8i			
	F			8o, 4i			
Combos	A/B				4	4	
	A/C		1			4	
	A/E			4			
	B/A						8
	B/C				4		
	B/D			2			4
	C/A		1			4	
	C/B				4		2
	C/D				4		2
	C/E		1				
	D/A		1	2			
	D/B			2			6
	D/C					4	
	E/B			2			
	E/F			4			
	F/B			4			
	F/E			4			

⌀ finished size

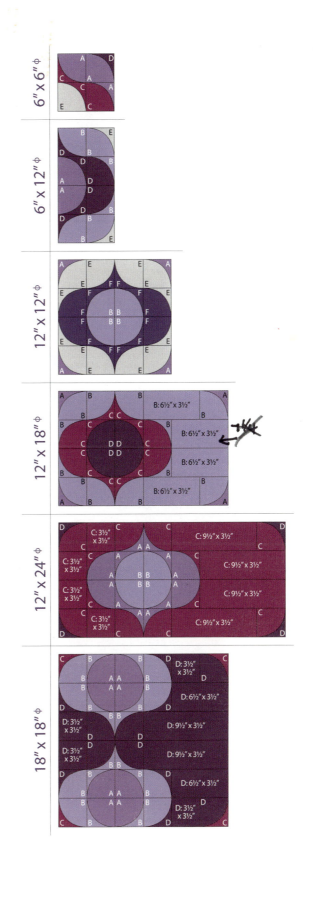

BLOCK 113: curva

-parallel
BLOCK 114

Assembly

Instructions are written for the 12" x 12" ⏀ block. Assembly for all blocks is similar. Use these instructions along with the cutting chart and diagrams to make your sized block.

1. Cut fabrics A, B and C as noted in the Cutting chart for your chosen block size.

2. Sew the center block of strips, alternating the B: 10½" x 1½", A: 10½" x 1½" and C: 10½" x 1½" strips. Press seams to one side.

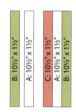

3. Sew two A: 5½" x 1½" strips to the top and bottom of the unit from the previous step. Press towards A.

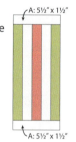

4. Sew one A: 12½" x 6½" to the left side of the unit from the previous step. Press towards A.

5. Sew one A: 12½" x 1½" to the right side of the unit from the previous step. Press towards A.

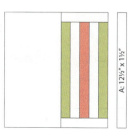

CUTTING		6"x6" ⏀	6"x12" ⏀	12"x12" ⏀	12"x18" ⏀	12"x24" ⏀	18"x18" ⏀
	Dimensions	**Quantity**					
A	1½" x 1½"	2	2				
	5½" x 1½"			2			
	6½" x 1½"	1					
	10½" x 1½"			2	6	8	
	12½" x 1½"		1	1	1	1	
	13½" x 1½"				2		2
	16½" x 1½"						6
	17½" x 1½"					2	
	18½" x 1½"						1
	6½" x 4½"	1					
	12½" x 4½"		1		1		
	18½" x 4½"						1
	12½" x 6½"			1		1	
B	4½" x 1½"	1					
	10½" x 1½"		1	2	4	5	
	16½" x 1½"						4
C	10½" x 1½"			1	3	4	
	16½" x 1½"						3

⏀ finished size

color, block & quilt

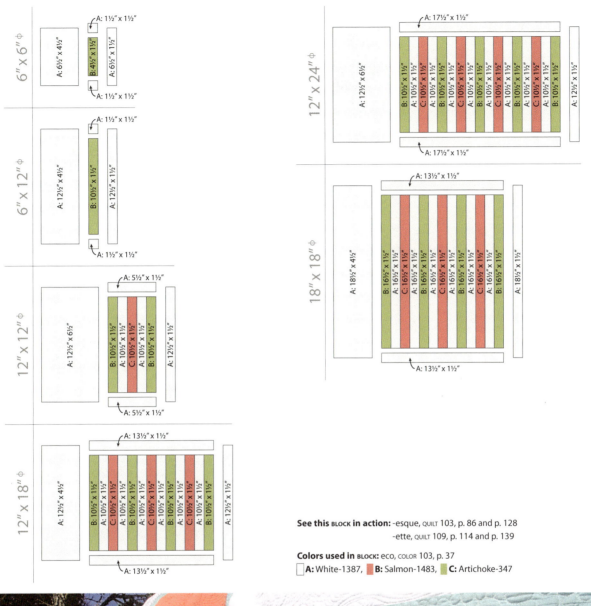

See this block in action: -esque, QUILT 103, p. 86 and p. 128
-ette, QUILT 109, p. 114 and p. 139

Colors used in block: eco, COLOR 103, p. 37
A: White-1387, **B:** Salmon-1483, **C:** Artichoke-347

BLOCK 114: -parallel

-codex
BLOCK 115

Assembly

Instructions are written for the 12" x 12" ᶲ block. Assembly for all blocks is similar. Use these instructions along with the cutting chart and diagrams to make your sized block.

1. Cut fabrics A-F as noted in the Cutting chart for your chosen block size.

2. Sew the pieces into strips. For the bottom row, sew the C and B squares together first, then sew the A: 4½" x 2½" and A: 8½" x 4½" to the left and right.

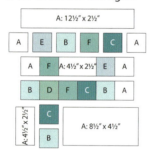

3. Sew the strips together, nesting seams in adjacent rows.

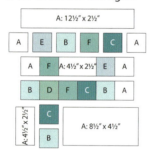

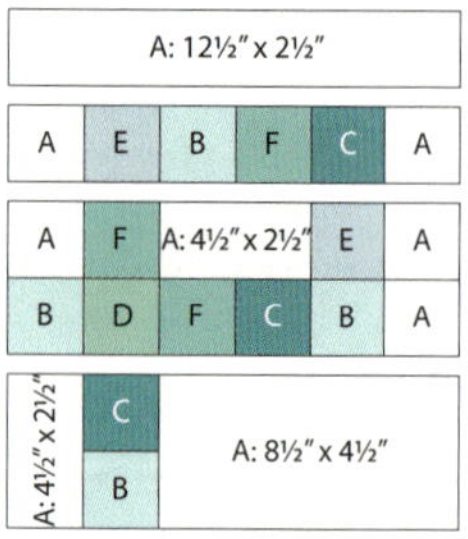

4. Press row seams to one side.

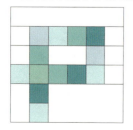

CUTTING	Dimensions	6"x6" ᶲ	6"x12" ᶲ	12"x12" ᶲ	12"x18" ᶲ	12"x24" ᶲ	18"x18" ᶲ
	Quantity						
A	2½" x 2½"	3	2	5	2	2	5
	4½" x 2½"			2	1	4	5
	6½" x 2½"	1					
	8½" x 2½"		1				1
	10½" x 2½"				1	1	
	12½" x 2½"			1	1	1	1
	14½" x 2½"						1
	4½" x 4½"				1		
	6½" x 4½"				1	1	
	8½" x 4½"			1		1	
	12½" x 4½"				1	1	1
	18½" x 4½"						1
B	2½" x 2½"		1	4	4	6	6
C	2½" x 2½"	1	1	3	4	6	5
D	2½" x 2½"		1	1	2	6	5
E	2½" x 2½"	1	1	2	3	3	3
F	2½" x 2½"	1	2	3	4	4	6

ᶲ finished size

See this block in action: -athon, QUILT 107, p. 104 and p. 134
-ette, QUILT 109, p. 114 and p. 139

Colors used in block: aqua, COLOR 104, p. 37
A: Bone-1037, **B:** Aqua-1005, **C:** Jade Green-1183, **D:** Pond-200, **E:** Dusty Blue-362, **F:** Candy Green-1061

color, block & quilt

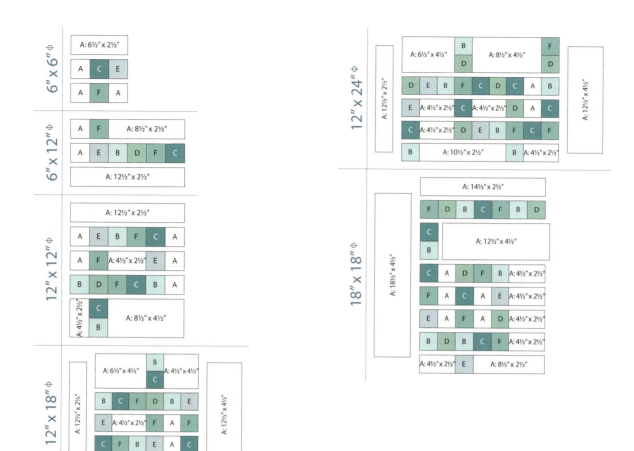

BLOCK 115: -codex

quilt

This section contains ten quilt templates to serve as a framework for your project, with perfectly-sized blanks where your chosen blocks will go. Sizes range from the wee tiny -ette, QUILT 109 (p. 114), which is perfect for babies, dolls and wallhangings, to the largest -esque, QUILT 103 (p. 86), perfect for a queen or king bed.

See a design you like, but in the wrong size? Here are some ideas to adapt your favorite design to the size you need:

-cosm, QUILT 101

bigger: Add another column of BLOCKS in the middle and enlarge the border.

smaller: Crop columns and rows.

-ruption, QUILT 102

bigger: Add borders in the background color and center column color (C).

smaller: Crop rows and borders.

-esque, QUILT 103

bigger: Add a small border in the background color (A) for king sized beds.

smaller: Crop entire quilt or consider QUILT 110.

-mania, QUILT 104

bigger: Add BLOCKS to rows. Add more rows.

smaller: Use smaller BLOCKS and adjust sashing.

-asaurus, QUILT 105

bigger: Add additional columns and/or rows of BLOCKS and solid blocks. Enlarge border.

smaller: Crop columns and rows or use smaller blocks and adjust sashing.

-scope, QUILT 106

bigger: Add additional columns and/or rows of BLOCKS and solid blocks. Adjust sashing and borders.

smaller: Crop columns and rows.

-athon, QUILT 107

bigger: Add borders in the background color and center background row (F).

-ism, QUILT 108

bigger: Add more BLOCKS to the block row. Adjust the strip lengths. Add more strips to the top and bottom.

-ette, QUILT 109

bigger: Scale up the entire quilt to use 12" x 12" or 18" x 18" BLOCKS.

-avore, QUILT 110

bigger: Make two -avore tops plus two mirror image -avore tops. Piece together an -avore mirror and -avore in the top row. Then an upside down -avore and -avore mirror in the bottom row.

QUILT:
contents

QUILT 101
-cosm
p. 78

QUILT 102
-ruption
p. 82

QUILT 103
-esque
p. 86

QUILT 104
-mania
p. 92

QUILT 105
-asaurus
p. 96

QUILT 106
-scope
p. 100

QUILT 107
-athon
p. 104

QUILT 108
-ism
p. 110

QUILT 109
-ette
p. 114

QUILT 110
-avore
p. 118

-cosm
QUILT 101

DIMENSIONS 52" x 67"
PIECING Emily Cier
QUILTING Angela Walters
APPENDIX omni-retro-cosm, p. 124

-cosm
QUILT 101

52" x 67"

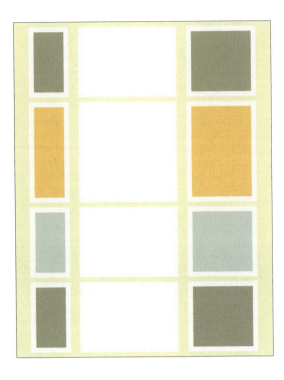

YARDAGE

A	1⅛ yards	
B	1 yard	
C	⅜ yard	
D	⅜ yard	
E	⅜ yard	
Batting	60" x 75"	
Backing	3½ yards	
Binding	⅝ yard	

BLOCKS

Dimensions	Quantity
12" x 18" ᵠ	3
18" x 18" ᵠ	1

ᵠ finished size

CUTTING

	First Cut		Second Cut	
	Dimensions	Quantity	Dimensions	Quantity
A	1½" x WOF	6	46½" x 1½" *	5
	2½" x WOF	4	14½" x 2½"	6
			20½" x 2½"	2
	3½" x WOF	4	34" x 3½"	4
B	1½" x WOF	19	8½" x 1½"	8
			12½" x 1½"	18
			14½" x 1½"	8
			18½" x 1½"	6
			20½" x 1½"	8
C	12½" x WOF	1	6½" x 12½"	2
			12½" x 12½"	2
D	12½" x WOF	1	6½" x 18½"	1
			12½" x 18½"	1
E	12½" x WOF	1	6½" x 12½"	1
			12½" x 12½"	1

* For strips longer than 40" wide, sew two strips together and then subcut the longer pieces.

Colors used in quilt: omni, color 110, p. 40
A: Zucchini-354, **B:** Oyster-1268, **C:** Sweet Pea-201, **D:** Ochre-1704, **E:** Seafoam-1328

Prep

1. Choose your palette from COLOR (pp. 32-43).
2. Choose your blocks from BLOCK (pp. 44-74).
3. Assemble your chosen blocks in your chosen color following the instructions in BLOCK (pp. 44-74).
4. Cut the Setting pieces using the chart to the left.

Assembly

1. Sew B strips of appropriate length to the left and right sides of each BLOCK. Repeat with the C, D, and E solid color blocks according to the assembly diagram. Press seams to the outside.

2. Sew the remaining B strips of appropriate length to the top and bottom of each BLOCK. Press seams to the outside.

color, block & quilt

3. Sew two A: 34" x 3½" pieces end-to-end to form one 67½" x 3½". Repeat for the other two A: 34" x 3½" pieces.

4. Start the top row by taking one BLOCK: 12" x 18" ᶲ (framed with B) and sewing an A: 14½" x 2½" piece on either side. Press towards A.

5. Sew one C: 6½" x 12½" (framed with B) and sew to the left of the unit from Step 4. Repeat on the right side with the C: 12½" x 12½" (framed with B). Press towards A.

6. Continue constructing the rows following the assembly diagram.

7. Sew all of the rows together, alternating the A: 46½" x 1½" strips with the strips of blocks, forming a single center column. *Note: Make sure the A: 14½" x 2½" pieces are aligned vertically when sewing the rows together.*

8. Sew the two A: 67½" x 3½" from Step 3 on either side. Press towards the outside.

Finishing

1. Layer your backing, batting and quilt top. Baste.
2. Quilt.
3. Trim, square corners and add binding.

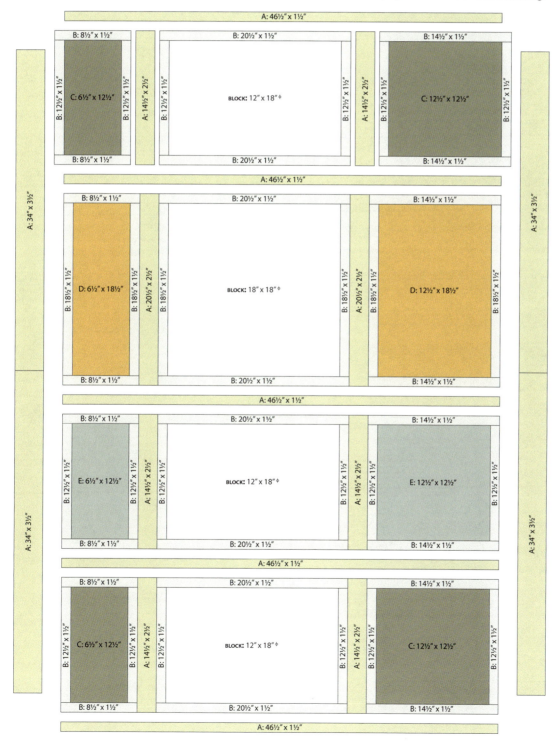

QUILT 101: -cosm 81

-ruption
QUILT 102

DIMENSIONS 65" x 78"
PIECING Emily Cier
QUILTING Angela Walters
APPENDIX super-auto-loco-ruption, p. 126

-ruption
QUILT 102

65" x 78"

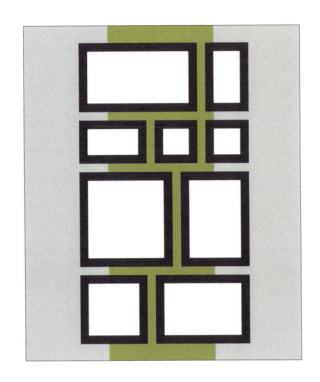

YARDAGE

	A	2 yards
	B	1½ yards
	C	¾ yard
	Batting	73" x 86"
	Backing	4⅞ yards
	Binding	⅝ yards

BLOCKS

Dimensions	Quantity
6" x 6" ⌀	2
6" x 12" ⌀	2
12" x 12" ⌀	1
12" x 18" ⌀	2
12" x 24" ⌀	1
18" x 18" ⌀	1

⌀ finished size

CUTTING

	First Cut		Second Cut	
	Dimensions	Quantity	Dimensions	Quantity
A	2½" x WOF	2	7½" x 2½"	6
A	4½" x WOF	1	7½" x 4½"	4
A	13½" x WOF	4	39½" x 13½"	4
B	2½" x WOF	17	6½" x 2½"	6
B			10½" x 2½"	6
B			12½" x 2½"	8
B			16½" x 2½"	6
B			18½" x 2½"	4
B			22½" x 2½"	4
B			28½" x 2½"	2
C	2½" x WOF	5	10½" x 2½"	2
C			16½" x 2½"	2
C			22½" x 2½"	1
C			26½" x 2½"	3
C	4½" x WOF	2	26½" x 4½"	2

Colors used in QUILT: super, COLOR 106, p. 38
A: Ash-1007, **B:** Charcoal-1071, **C:** Olive-1263

color, block & quilt

Prep

1. Choose your palette from COLOR (pp. 32-43).
2. Choose your blocks from BLOCK (pp. 44-74).
3. Assemble your chosen blocks in your chosen color following the instructions in BLOCK (pp. 44-74).
4. Cut the Setting pieces using the chart on the opposite page.

Assembly

1. Sew B strips of appropriate lengths to the left and right sides of each BLOCK according to the assembly diagram. Press seams toward B.

2. Sew the remaining B strips to the top and bottom of each BLOCK. Press seams toward B.

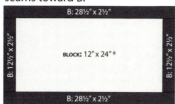

3. Sew two A: 39½" x 13½" pieces end-to-end to form one 78½" x 13½". Repeat for the other two A: 39½" x 13½" pieces. Press seams to one side.
4. Sew the top row by taking one C: 26½" x 4½" and sewing a A: 7½" x 4½" on either side. Press towards A.
5. Sew the next row by taking one BLOCK: 12" x 24" ɸ and one BLOCK: 6" x 12" ɸ (both framed with B) and sewing them on either side of a C: 16½" x 2½". Press towards C.
6. Continue constructing the rows following the assembly diagram.
7. Sew all of the rows together, forming a single center column. Press seams to one side.
8. Sew the two A: 78½" x 13½" from Step 3 on either side. Press toward A.

Finishing

1. Layer your backing, batting and quilt top. Baste.
2. Quilt.
3. Trim, square corners and add binding.

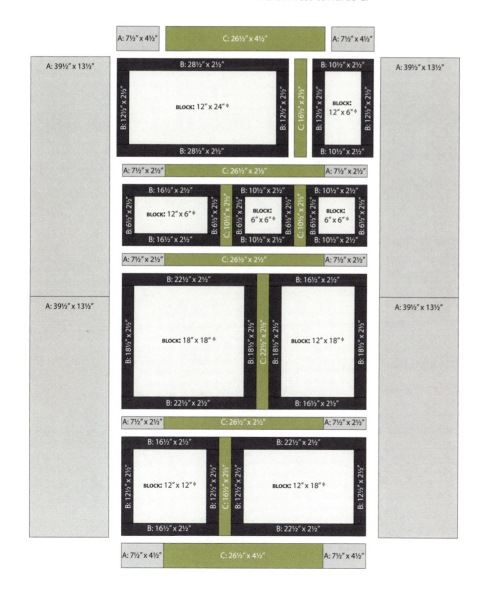

QUILT 102: -ruption

-esque
QUILT 103

DIMENSIONS 103" x 98"
PIECING Emily Cier
QUILTING Angela Walters
APPENDIX eco-parallel-esque, p. 128 *(opposite page)*
paleo-domus-esque, p. 129

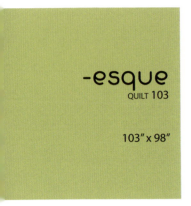

-esque
QUILT 103

103" x 98"

YARDAGE

A	4⅜ yards
B	1⅝ yards
C	1⅛ yards
D	1⅛ yards
E	1½ yards
F	2⅛ yards
Batting	111" x 106"
Backing	9 yards
Binding	1 yard

BLOCKS

Dimensions	Quantity
6" x 6" ◊	1
6" x 12" ◊	4
12" x 12" ◊	1
12" x 18" ◊	3
12" x 24" ◊	1
18" x 18" ◊	2

◊ finished size

color, block & quilt

CUTTING

	First Cut		Second Cut	
	Dimensions	**Quantity**	**Dimensions**	**Quantity**
A	1½" x WOF	32	6½" x 1½"	5
			12½" x 1½"	11
			18½" x 1½"	5
			25½" x 1½"	1
			31½" x 1½"	3
			37½" x 1½"	3
			44½" x 1½" *	1
			51½" x 1½" *	11
			98½" x 1½" *	1
	6½" x WOF	5	5½" x 6½"	1
			6½" x 6½"	1
			25½" x 6½"	1
			32½" x 6½"	1
			37½" x 6½"	1
			39½" x 6½"	2
	7½" x WOF	6	12½" x 7½"	2
			18½" x 7½"	1
			31½" x 7½"	1
			44½" x 7½" *	1
			51½" x 7½" *	1
	12½" x WOF	1	13½" x 12½"	1
B	6½" x WOF	1	6½" x 6½"	3
	12½" x WOF	1	12½" x 12½"	1
			12½" x 24½"	1
	18½" x WOF	1	18½" x 18½"	1
C	12½" x WOF	2	6½" x 12½"	1
			12½" x 12½"	2
			12½" x 18½"	1
D	12½" x WOF	2	12½" x 24½"	2
E	12½" x WOF	3	6½" x 12½"	2
			12½" x 12½"	1
			12½" x 18½"	1
			12½" x 24½"	2
F	12½" x WOF	3	6½" x 12½"	1
			12½" x 18½"	3
			12½" x 24½"	1
	18½" x WOF	1	18½" x 18½"	1

* For strips longer than 40" wide, sew two strips together and then subcut the longer pieces.

Prep

1. Choose your palette from COLOR (pp. 32-43).
2. Choose your blocks from BLOCK (pp. 44-74).
3. Assemble your chosen blocks in your chosen color following the instructions in BLOCK (pp. 44-74).
4. Cut the Setting pieces using the chart to the left.

Assembly

1. First, sew each of the basic groups together according to the illustrations on pp. 90-91. Press as needed throughout each step.
2. Sew each pair of groups split by a - - 2 - - line.
3. Sew each pair of groups split by a - - 3 - - line.
4. Sew each pair of groups split by a - - 4 - - line.
5. Sew each pair of groups split by a - - 5 - - line.
6. Sew each pair of groups split by a - - 6 - - line.

Finishing

1. Layer your backing, batting and quilt top. Baste.
2. Quilt.
3. Trim, square corners and add binding.

Colors used in QUILT: eco, COLOR 103, p. 37
A: Aqua-1005, **B:** Zucchini-354, **C:** Salmon-1483,
D: Artichoke-347, **E:** White-1387, **F:** Mushroom-1239

QUILT 103: -esque

-mania
QUILT 104

DIMENSIONS 40" x 50"
PIECING Emily Cier
QUILTING Angela Walters
APPENDIX geo-macro-flora-mania, p. 130

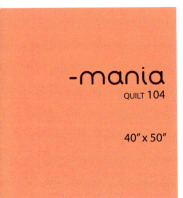

-mania
QUILT 104

40" x 50"

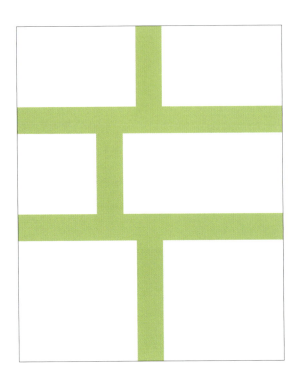

YARDAGE

	A	¾ yard
	Batting	48" x 58"
	Backing	2¾ yards
	Binding	½ yard

BLOCKS

Dimensions	Quantity
12" x 12" ⁕	1
12" x 18" ⁕	2
12" x 24" ⁕	1
18" x 18" ⁕	2

⁕ finished size

CUTTING

	First Cut		Second Cut	
	Dimensions	Quantity	Dimensions	Quantity
A	4½" x WOF	4	12½" x 4½"	2
			18½" x 4½"	1
			40½" x 4½"	2

94 color, block & quilt

Prep

1. Choose your palette from COLOR (pp. 32-43).
2. Choose your blocks from BLOCK (pp. 44-74).
3. Assemble your chosen blocks in your chosen color following the instructions in BLOCK (pp. 44-74).
4. Cut the Setting pieces using the chart on the opposite page.

Assembly

1. Sew the top row by taking one A: 12½" x 4½" and sewing a BLOCK: 12" x 18"◊ on either side. Press towards A.
2. Sew the middle and bottom rows similarly according to the diagram.
3. Sew all of the rows together, alternating with A: 40½" x 4½" strips. Press towards A.

Finishing

1. Layer your backing, batting and quilt top. Baste.
2. Quilt.
3. Trim, square corners and add binding.

Color used in QUILT: geo, COLOR 105, p. 38
A: Sprout-254

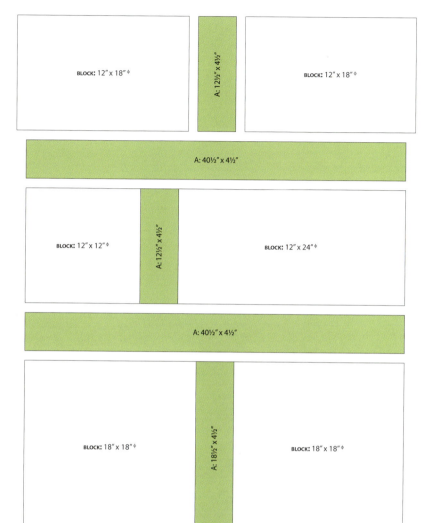

QUILT 104: -mania 95

-asaurus
QUILT 105

DIMENSIONS 86" x 84"
PIECING Emily Cier
QUILTING Angela Walters
APPENDIX trans-poly-asaurus, p. 132 *(opposite page)*
luma-tele-asaurus, p. 131

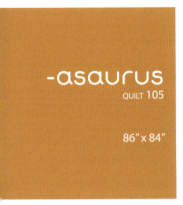

-asaurus
QUILT 105

86" x 84"

YARDAGE

A	2⅜ yards
B	¾ yard
C	1⅛ yards
D	¾ yard
Batting	94" x 92"
Backing	7¾ yards
Binding	¾ yards

BLOCKS

Dimensions	Quantity
12" x 24" ⌀	11

⌀ finished size

CUTTING

	First Cut		Second Cut	
	Dimensions	Quantity	Dimensions	Quantity
A	1½" x WOF	4	38½" x 1½"	4
	2½" x WOF	14	12½" x 2½"	12
			38½" x 2½"	10
	5½" x WOF	5	84½" x 5½" *	2
B	12½" x WOF	2	24½" x 12½"	2
C	12½" x WOF	3	24½" x 12½"	3
D	12½" x WOF	2	24½" x 12½"	2

* For strips longer than 40" wide, sew multiple strips together and then subcut the longer pieces.

Prep

1. Choose your palette from COLOR (pp. 32-43).

2. Choose your blocks from BLOCK (pp. 44-74).

3. Assemble your chosen blocks in your chosen color following the instructions in BLOCK (pp. 44-74).

4. Cut the Setting pieces using the chart above.

Assembly

1. Start the top row by taking one B: 24½" x 12½" and sewing an A: 12½" x 2½" on the right side. Press towards A.

2. Sew the one BLOCK: 12" x 24" ⌀ to the right side of the unit from the previous step. Press towards A.

3. Continue sewing the first row and all the subsequent rows according to the assembly diagram.

4. Sew two A: 38½" x 2½" pieces end-to-end to form one 76½" x 2½". Repeat for the other remaining A: 38½" x 2½" pieces. Repeat the same process for the A: 38½" x 1½" pieces. Press all seams to one side.

5. Sew all of the rows together, alternating the rows with the pieced A: 76½" x 2½" strips. Press towards A. *Note: Make sure the A: 12½" x 2½" pieces are aligned vertically when sewing the rows together.*

color, block & quilt

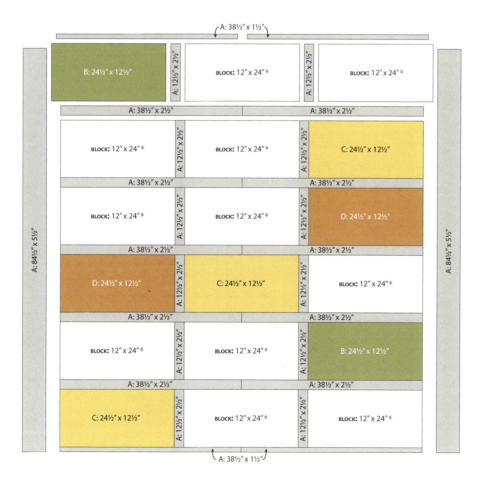

6. Sew the two A: 76½" x 1½" on the top and bottom. Press towards A.
7. Sew the two A: 84½" x 5½" on the left and right. Press towards A.

Finishing

1. Layer your backing, batting and quilt top. Baste.
2. Quilt.
3. Trim, square corners and add binding.

Colors used in quilt: trans, color 107, p. 39
A: Parchment-413, **B:** Olive-1263, **C:** Corn Yellow-1089, **D:** Amber-1479

quilt 105: -asaurus

-scope
QUILT 106

DIMENSIONS 43" x 50"
PIECING Emily Cier
QUILTING Angela Walters
APPENDIX terra-pluvia-scope, p. 125

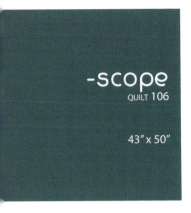

-scope
QUILT 106

43" x 50"

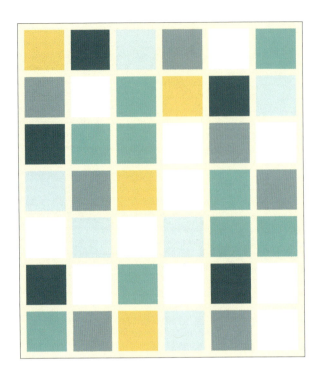

YARDAGE

	A	⅞ yard
	B	⅜ yard
	C	⅜ yard
	D	⅜ yard
	E	⅜ yard
	F	⅜ yard
	Batting	51" x 58"
	Backing	2⅞ yards
	Binding	½ yards

BLOCKS

Dimensions	Quantity
6" x 6" ⏀	11

⏀ finished size

CUTTING

	First Cut		Second Cut	
	Dimensions	Quantity	Dimensions	Quantity
A	1½" x WOF	18	6½" x 1½"	35
			41½" x 1½" *	8
			50½" x 1½" *	2
B	6½" x WOF	1	6½" x 6½"	4
C	6½" x WOF	1	6½" x 6½"	5
D	6½" x WOF	1	6½" x 6½"	6
E	6½" x WOF	2	6½" x 6½"	7
F	6½" x WOF	2	6½" x 6½"	9

* For strips longer than 40" wide, sew two strips together and then subcut the longer pieces.

Colors used in QUILT: terra, COLOR 101, p. 36
A: Maize-1216, **B:** Sunflower-353, **C:** Emerald-1135,
D: Ice Frappe-1173, **E:** Sage-1321, **F:** Candy Green-1061

color, block & quilt

Prep

1. Choose your palette from COLOR (pp. 32-43).
2. Choose your blocks from BLOCK (pp. 44-74).
3. Assemble your chosen blocks in your chosen color following the instructions in BLOCK (pp. 44-74).
4. Cut the Setting pieces using the chart on the opposite page.

Assembly

1. Sew the top row by taking one B: 6½" x 6½" and sewing an A: 6½" x 1½" on the right side. Press towards A.
2. Sew the one C: 6½" x 6½" to the right side of the unit above.
3. Continue sewing the first row and all the subsequent rows according to the assembly diagram.
4. Sew all of the rows together, alternating the rows with A: 41½" x 1½" strips. Press towards A. *Note: Make sure the A: 6½" x 1½" sashing pieces are aligned vertically when sewing the rows together.*
5. Sew the two A: 50½" x 1½" on either side. Press towards A.

Finishing

1. Layer your backing, batting and quilt top. Baste.
2. Quilt.
3. Trim, square corners and add binding.

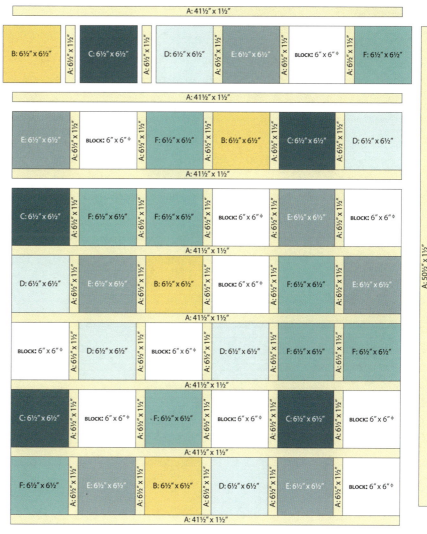

QUILT 106: -scope

-athon
QUILT 107

DIMENSIONS 65" x 78"
PIECING Emily Cier
QUILTING Angela Walters
APPENDIX aqua-coden-athon, p. 134 *(opposite page)*
florus-orbis-athon, p. 135

-athon
QUILT 107

60" x 70"

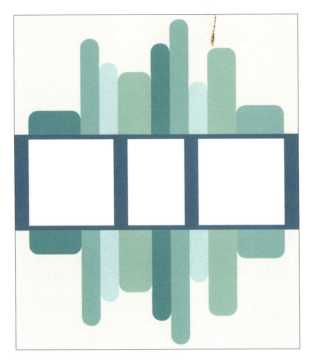

YARDAGE

	A	2 yards
	B	⅝ yard
	C	¾ yard
	D	½ yard
	E	¾ yard
	F	½ yard
	Batting	68" x 78"
	Backing	3⅞ yards
	Binding	⅝ yards

BLOCKS

Dimensions	Quantity
12" x 18" ⏀	1
18" x 18" ⏀	2

⏀ finished size

color, block & quilt

Prep

1. Choose your palette from COLOR (pp. 32-43).
2. Choose your blocks from BLOCK (pp. 44-74).
3. Assemble your chosen blocks in your chosen color following the instructions in BLOCK (pp. 44-74).
4. Cut the Setting pieces using the chart to the right.

Assembly

1. Cut and assemble the quantity of **Quarter Curve – 2"** blocks listed in the Cutting Chart on p. 108 using the instructions on p. 30.
2. Construct each of the columns in the upper and lower portions of the quilt following the diagram on p. 109. For example, the first pieced column in the top portion, sew two A/B Quarter Curves on either side of B: 7½" x 2½". Press towards the center. Sew a B: 11½" x 3½" and an A: 20½" x 11½" on either side. Press towards the outside.
3. Sew the columns together to form the top and bottom. Press seams to one side.
4. Sew the central row of F: 18½" x 3½" and BLOCKS following the diagram on p. 109. Press towards F. Sew two F: 60½" x 1½" to the top and bottom. Press towards F.
5. Sew the three sections together. Press towards F.

Finishing

1. Layer your backing, batting and quilt top. Baste.
2. Quilt.
3. Trim, square corners and add binding.

Colors used in BLOCK: aqua, COLOR 104, p. 37
 A: Bone-1037, **B:** Jade Green-1183, **C:** Candy Green-1061,
 D: Aqua-1005, **E:** Pond-200, **F:** Caribbean-1064

CUTTING

	First Cut		Second Cut	
	Dimensions	Quantity	Dimensions	Quantity
A	3½" x WOF	4	25½" x 3½"	4
	4½" x WOF	2	1½" x 4½"	2
			5½" x 4½"	2
			6½" x 4½"	2
			10½" x 4½"	2
			14½" x 4½"	2
	7½" x WOF	1	7½" x 6½"	2
			12½" x 7½"	2
	10½" x WOF	1	19½" x 10½"	2
	11½" x WOF	2	20½" x 11½"	2
B	2½" x WOF	1	7½" x 2½"	2
	3½" x WOF	1	11½" x 3½"	2
	4½" x WOF	1	17½" x 4½"	2
C	2½" x WOF	1	6½" x 2½"	2
	4½" x WOF	3	10½" x 4½"	2
			18½" x 4½"	2
			22½" x 4½"	2
D	4½" x WOF	2	9½" x 4½"	2
			13½" x 4½"	2
E	2½" x WOF	1	2½" x 2½"	2
			2½" x 3½"	2
	6½" x WOF	1	16½" x 6½"	2
	7½" x WOF	1	11½" x 7½"	2
F	1½" x WOF	4	60½" x 1½" *	2
	3½" x WOF	2	18½" x 3½"	4

* For strips longer than 40" wide, sew two strips together and then subcut the longer pieces.

QUILT 107: -athon

Quarter Curve – 2"			
Strips		A	3
		B	1
		C	1
		D	1
		E	1
Inner(i)/Outer(o) Curves		A	36o
		B	8i
		C	12i
		D	8i
		E	8i
Combos	A/B		8
	A/C		12
	A/D		8
	A/E		8

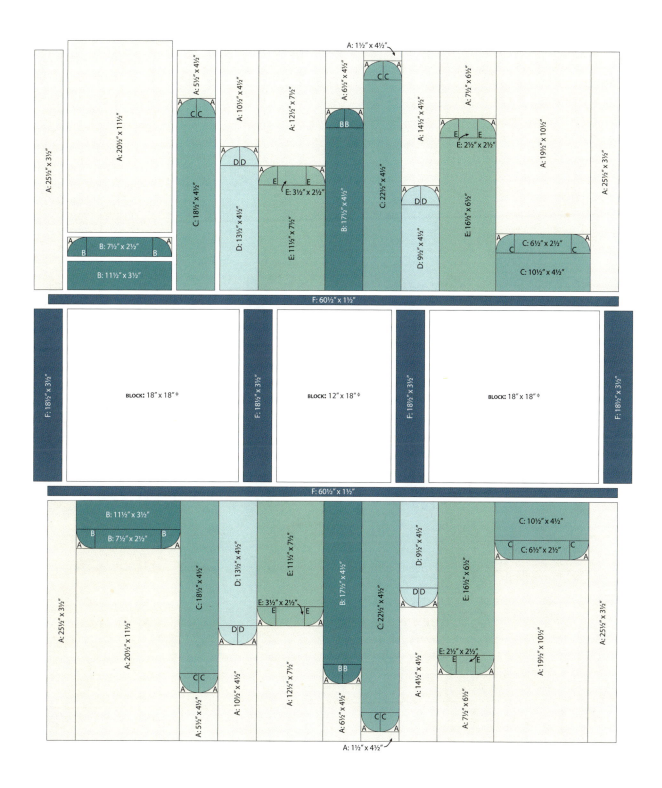

QUILT 107: -athon

-ism
QUILT 108

DIMENSIONS 50" x 50"
PIECING Emily Cier
QUILTING Angela Walters
APPENDIX inter-proto-ism, p. 137 *(opposite page)*
lapis-curva-ism, p. 136

-ism
QUILT 108

50" x 50"

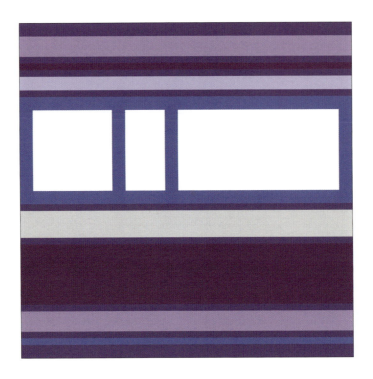

YARDAGE

	A	¾ yard
	B	½ yard
	C	⅞ yard
	D	¼ yard
	E	½ yard
	F	⅜ yard
	Batting	58" x 58"
	Backing	3⅜ yards
	Binding	½ yards

BLOCKS

Dimensions	Quantity
6" x 12" ⌀	1
12" x 12" ⌀	1
12" x 24" ⌀	1

⌀ finished size

CUTTING

	First Cut		Second Cut	
	Dimensions	Quantity	Dimensions	Quantity
A	1½" x WOF	10	50½" x 1½" *	7
	2½" x WOF	3	50½" x 2½" *	2
B	3½" x WOF	3	50½" x 3½" *	2
C	1½" x WOF	2	50½" x 1½" *	1
	9½" x WOF	2	50½" x 9½" *	1
D	2½" x WOF	2	50½" x 2½" *	1
E	1½" x WOF	2	50½" x 1½" *	1
	2½" x WOF	4	12½" x 2½"	4
			50½" x 2½" *	2
F	4½" x WOF	2	50½" x 4½" *	1

* For strips longer than 40" wide, sew two strips together and then subcut the longer pieces.

Prep

1. Choose your palette from COLOR (pp. 32-43).
2. Choose your blocks from BLOCK (pp. 44-74).
3. Assemble your chosen blocks in your chosen color following the instructions in BLOCK (pp. 44-74).
4. Cut the Setting pieces using the chart above.

Assembly

1. Sew the horizontal strips together in the order shown in the assembly diagram. Press seams to one side.
2. When you reach the block row, alternate sewing the E: 12½" x 2½" pieces with the BLOCKS. Press towards E.
3. Continue sewing the rows together until the quilt top is complete.

color, block & quilt

Finishing

1. Layer your backing, batting and quilt top. Baste.
2. Quilt.
3. Trim, square corners and add binding.

Colors used in quilt: lapis, color 114, p. 42
- **A:** Tulip-327, **B:** Wisteria-1392, **C:** Dark Violet-1485,
- **D:** Lavender-1189, **E:** Lapis-357, **E:** Ash-1007

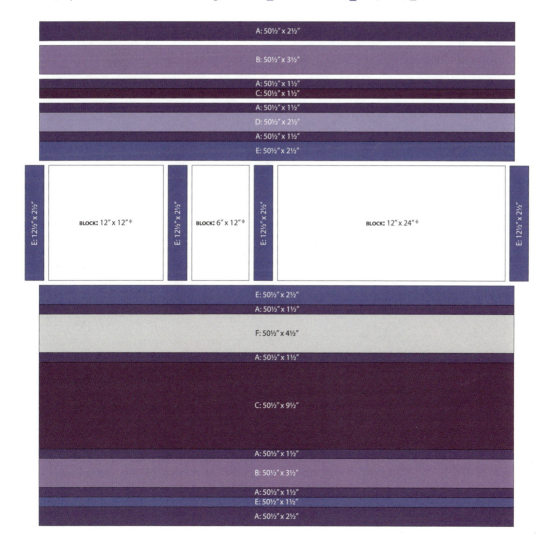

QUILT 108: -ism

-ette
QUILT 109

DIMENSIONS 30" x 30"
PIECING Emily Cier
QUILTING Angela Walters
APPENDIX lux-curva-ette, p. 138 *(opposite page)*
nano-poly-ette, p. 139

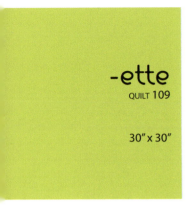

-ette
QUILT 109

30" x 30"

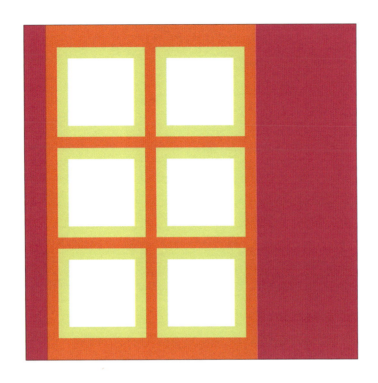

YARDAGE

A	½ yard
B	⅜ yard
C	⅜ yard
Batting	38" x 38"
Backing	1⅛ yards
Binding	⅜ yards

BLOCKS

Dimensions	Quantity
6" x 6" ᶲ	6

ᶲ finished size

CUTTING

	First Cut		Second Cut	
	Dimensions	Quantity	Dimensions	Quantity
A	2½" x WOF	1	30½" x 2½"	1
	9½" x WOF	1	30½" x 9½"	1
B	1½" x WOF	4	8½" x 1½"	9
			19½" x 1½"	2
	2½" x WOF	1	19½" x 2½"	2
C	1½" x WOF	5	6½" x 1½"	12
			8½" x 1½"	12

Prep

1. Choose your palette from COLOR (pp. 32-43).
2. Choose your blocks from BLOCK (pp. 44-74).
3. Assemble your chosen blocks in your chosen color following the instructions in BLOCK (pp. 44-74).
4. Cut the Setting pieces using the chart above.

Assembly

1. Sew C: 6½" x 1½" strips to the left and right sides of each BLOCK. Press seams towards C.
2. Sew C: 8½" x 1½" strips to the top and bottom of each unit from the previous step. Press seams towards C.
3. Construct each row, alternating B: 8½" x 1½" pieces with two framed BLOCKS. Press towards B. Repeat for the remaining BLOCKS.

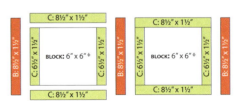

116 color, block & quilt

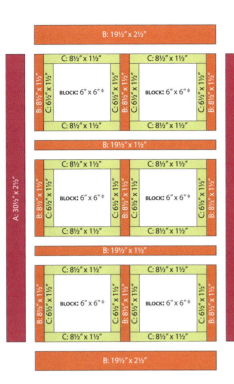

4. Sew the rows together, alternating them with the B: 19½" x 2½" and B: 19½" x 1½" pieces as shown. Press towards B. *Note: Make sure the B: 8½" x 1½" sashing pieces are aligned vertically when sewing the rows together.*

5. Sew the A: 30½" x 2½" piece to the left side. Sew the A: 30½" x 9½" piece to the right side. Press towards A.

Finishing

1. Layer your backing, batting and quilt top. Baste.
2. Quilt.
3. Trim, square corners and add binding.

Colors used in QUILT: nano, COLOR 112, p. 41
A: Pomegranate-1295, **B:** Kumquat-410, **C:** Cactus-199

-avore
QUILT 110

DIMENSIONS 31" x 40"
PIECING Emily Cier
QUILTING Angela Walters
APPENDIX circum-poly-avore, p. 140

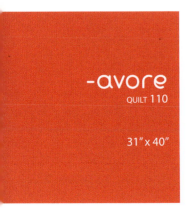

-avore
QUILT 110

31" x 40"

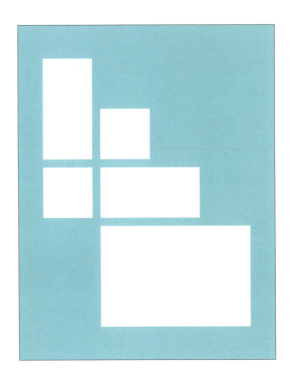

YARDAGE

	A	1¾ yards
	Batting	39" x 48"
	Backing	1⅜ yards
	Binding	⅜ yards

BLOCKS

Dimensions	Quantity
6" x 6" ⌽	2
6" x 12" ⌽	2
12" x 18" ⌽	1

⌽ finished size

CUTTING

	First Cut		Second Cut	
	Dimensions	Quantity	Dimensions	Quantity
A	1½" x WOF	2	6½" x 1½"	2
			19½" x 1½"	2
	3½" x WOF	1	8½" x 3½"	1
			12½" x 3½"	1
			16½" x 3½"	1
	4½" x WOF	1	16½" x 4½"	1
			18½" x 4½"	1
	6½" x WOF	1	7½" x 6½"	1
	8½" x WOF	1	9½" x 8½"	1
	16½" x WOF	1	10½" x 16½"	1
			15½" x 16½"	1

Prep

1. Choose your palette from COLOR (pp. 32-43).
2. Choose your blocks from BLOCK (pp. 44-74).
3. Assemble your chosen blocks in your chosen color following the instructions in BLOCK (pp. 44-74).
4. Cut the Setting pieces using the chart on the opposite page.

Assembly

1. First, sew each of the basic groups together according to the illustrations on the following page. Press as needed throughout each step.
2. Sew each pair of groups split by a - - 2 - - line.
3. Sew each pair of groups split by a - - 3 - - line.
4. Sew each pair of groups split by a - - 4 - - line.
5. Sew each pair of groups split by a - - 5 - - line.
6. Sew each pair of groups split by a - - 6 - - line.

Finishing

1. Layer your backing, batting and quilt top. Baste.
2. Quilt.
3. Trim, square corners and add binding.

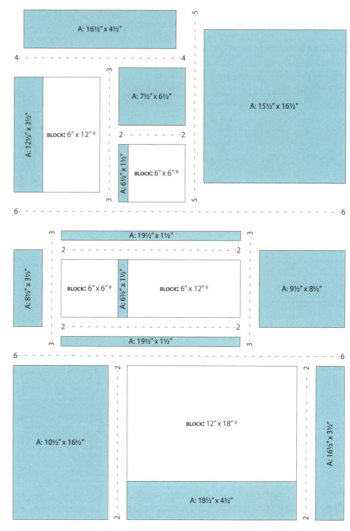

Color used in QUILT: circum, COLOR 102, p. 36
A: Azure-1009

QUILT 110: -avore

APPENDIX A:
I Want That Exact Quilt

The point of COLOR, BLOCK & QUILT is the infinite variety of quilts that you can create using just these few building blocks. But what if, by chance, you've fallen in love with one of the specific combinations pictured as examples in these pages? What then? Well, I'm happy to say you're in luck, because the appendix you find before you takes each of these examples, pulls together the yardage charts, colors, and other details that go into its component parts, and bakes them into a straight-up pattern to make the exact quilts pictured throughout the book.

Each pattern in this section contains a yardage chart and a cutting chart. The yardage chart contains all the fabric needed for the blocks, quilt, backing and binding. The cutting charts are for the blocks only. You will need to refer to the QUILTS section for the cutting chart for the corresponding quilt.

The letters used to designate individual colors often won't be the same from block to block or from block to quilt. Make sure to note the Block Color Assignments in the sidebar of each project and the Quilt Color Assignments in step 2 of the Assembly Instructions.

Follow the diagram in the sidebar for block placement and orientation when assembling your quilt top.

WARNING: The charts in this section are rather intimidating. Intense, even. It will take some time to work through and cut all the pieces in the huge cutting chart. If you want to Make That Exact Quilt, you'll find these charts will simplify your life a bit in the long run — but you've been warned.

As for the other 2,206,264,748,501,235, well, these are left as an exercise to the reader. First one to finish wins!

APPENDIX A:
contents

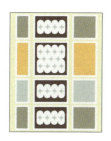
**omni
-retro
-cosm**
p. 124

**geo
-macro
-flora
-mania**
p. 130

**lapis
-curva
-ism**
p. 136

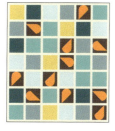
**terra
-pluvia
-scope**
p. 125

**luma
-tele
-asaurus**
p. 131

**inter
-proto
-ism**
p. 137

**super
-auto
-loco
-ruption**
p. 126

**trans
-poly
-asaurus**
p. 132

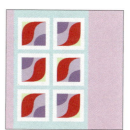
**lux
-curva
-ette**
p. 138

**eco
-parallel
-esque**
p. 128

**aqua
-codex
-athon**
p. 134

**nano
-poly
-ette**
p. 139

**paleo
-domus
-esque**
p. 129

**florus
-orbis
-athon**
p. 135

**circum
-poly
-avore**
p. 140

APPENDIX A: i want that exact quilt 123

omni-retro-cosm

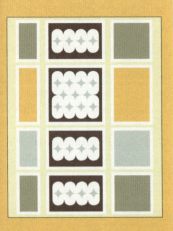

YARDAGE: Blocks & Setting

Zucchini-354	1⅛ yards	Batting	60" x 75"
Oyster-1268	1⅞ yards	Backing: Zucchini-354	3½ yards
Sweet Pea-201	⅜ yard		
Ochre-1704	⅜ yard	Binding: Cappuccino-406	⅝ yard (7 strips)
Seafoam-1328	⅞ yard		
Cappuccino-406	1 yard		

Assembly

1. Cut and assemble the blocks listed in the Details chart (4 total) in the specified sizes. A combined cutting chart and block color assignments are below and assembly instructions are on p. 64.

2. Construct -cosm, QUILT 101, following the cutting chart and instructions on p. 78 using colors **A:** Zucchini-354, **B:** Oyster-1268, **C:** Sweet Pea-201, **D:** Ochre-1704, **E:** Seafoam-1328.

CUTTING: Blocks

	First Cut		Second Cut	
	Dimensions	Quantity	Dimensions	Quantity
Cappuccino	1½" x WOF	4	12½" x 1½"	6
			16½" x 1½"	2
			18½" x 1½"	2
	2½" x WOF	3	16½" x 2½"	6

BLOCK 110: Quarter Curve – 2"

Strips	**A:** Cappuccino-406	5
	B: Oyster-1268	10
	C: Seafoam-1328	6
Curves †	**A:** Cappuccino-406	68**o**
	B: Oyster-1268	160**i**
	C: Seafoam-1328	92**o**
Combos	A/B	68
	C/B	92

† Inner (**i**)/Outer (**o**) Curves

details

COLOR	110 p. 40	omni	
BLOCK		size	quantity
	110 p. 64	12" x 18" ϕ	3
		18" x 18" ϕ	1
QUILT	101 p. 78	-cosm 52" x 67"	

ϕ finished size

block color assignments

BLOCK 110: retro
A: Cappuccino-406
B: Oyster-1268
C: Seafoam-1328

terra-pluvia-scope

YARDAGE: Blocks & Setting

Maize-1216	⅞ yards	Cappuccino-406	¾ yard
Sunflower-353	⅜ yard	**Batting**	51" x 58"
Emerald-1135	⅜ yard	**Backing:** Maize-1216	2⅞ yards
Ice Frappe-1173	⅜ yard		
Sage-1321	⅜ yard	**Binding:** Emerald-1135	½ yard (5 strips)
Candy Green-1061	⅜ yard		
School Bus-1482	½ yard		

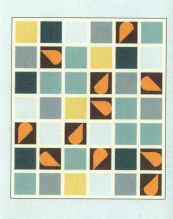

Assembly

1. Cut and assemble the blocks listed in the Details chart (11 total) in the specified sizes. A combined cutting chart and block color assignments are below and assembly instructions are on p. 52.

2. Construct -scope, QUILT 106, following the cutting chart and instructions on p. 100 using colors **A:** Maize-1216, **B:** Sunflower-353, **C:** Emerald-1135, **D:** Ice Frappe-1173, **E:** Sage-1321, **F:** Candy Green-1061.

details

COLOR	101 p. 36	terra	
		size	quantity
BLOCK	104 p. 52	6" x 6" ⌀	11
QUILT	106 p. 100	-scope 43" x 50"	

⌀ finished size

block color assignments

BLOCK 104: -pluvia
A: Cappuccino-406
B: School Bus-1482

CUTTING: Blocks

	First Cut		Second Cut	
	Dimensions	Quantity	Dimensions	Quantity
Cappuccino	1½" x WOF	4	6½" x 1½"	22
	2½" x WOF	1	2½" x 2½"	11
School Bus	2½" x WOF	1	2½" x 2½"	11

BLOCK 104: Quarter Curve – 2"		
Strips	**A:** Cappuccino-406	2
	B: School Bus-1482	2
†	**A:** Cappuccino-406	22**o**
	B: School Bus-1482	22**i**
‡		22

† Inner **(i)**/Outer **(o)** Curves
‡ Combos

BLOCK 104: Half-Square Triangle – 2"		
Strips	**A:** Cappuccino-406	1
	B: School Bus-1482	1
Squares	**A:** Cappuccino-406	11
	B: School Bus-1482	11
*		11
**		22

* Combos
** HST

super-auto-loco-ruption

YARDAGE: Blocks & Setting

Snow-1339	1 yard	Charcoal-1071	1⅜ yards
Olive-1263	1⅜ yards	**Batting**	73" x 86"
Candy Green-1061	½ yard	**Backing:** Ice Frappe-1173	4⅞ yards
Cactus-199	⅜ yard		
Ice Frappe-1173	⅜ yard	**Binding:** Charcoal-1071	⅝ yard (8 strips)
Ash-1007	2⅜ yards		

Assembly

1. Cut and assemble the blocks listed in the Details chart (9 total) in the specified sizes. A combined cutting chart is on the opposite page, block color assignments are below and assembly instructions are on p. 54 (BLOCK 105) and p. 56 (BLOCK 106).

2. Construct -ruption, QUILT 102, following the cutting chart and instructions on p. 82 using colors **A:** Ash-1007, **B:** Charcoal-1071, **C:** Olive-1263.

details

COLOR	106 p. 38	super	
		size	quantity
BLOCK	105 p. 54	6"x 6"◊	1
		6"x 12"◊	1
		12"x 18"◊	1
		18"x 18"◊	1
	106 p. 56	6"x 6"◊	1
		6"x 12"◊	1
		12"x 12"◊	1
		12"x 18"◊	1
		12"x 24"◊	1
QUILT	102 p. 82	-ruption 65"x 78"	

◊ finished size

block color assignments

BLOCK 105: -loco
- **A:** Snow-1339
- **B:** Olive-1263
- **C:** Candy Green-1061
- **D:** Cactus-199
- **E:** Ice Frappe-1173

BLOCK 106: -auto
- **A:** Snow-1339
- **B:** Candy Green-1061
- **C:** Ash-1007
- **D:** Olive-1263
- **E:** Cactus-199

CUTTING: Blocks

	First Cut		Second Cut	
	Dimensions	Quantity	Dimensions	Quantity
Snow	1½" x WOF	7	2½" x 1½"	1
			3½" x 1½"	1
			5½" x 1½"	1
			6½" x 1½"	3
			9½" x 1½"	3
			10½" x 1½"	3
			11½" x 1½"	3
			12½" x 1½"	7
	2½" x WOF	5	2½" x 2½"	15
			4½" x 2½"	12
			6½" x 2½"	8
			10½" x 2½"	1
			12½" x 2½"	2
Candy Green	2½" x WOF	2	2½" x 2½"	4
			10½" x 2½"	1
			12½" x 2½"	2
			14½" x 2½"	1
	4½" x WOF	1	4½" x 4½"	4
Ash	1½" x WOF	1	12½" x 1½"	1
	2½" x WOF	1	3½" x 2½"	1
			5½" x 2½"	1
	3½" x WOF	2	6½" x 3½"	4
			9½" x 3½"	3
Olive	1½" x WOF	2	6½" x 1½"	1
			10½" x 1½"	3
			11½" x 1½"	3
	2½" x WOF	1	2½" x 2½"	3
			4½" x 2½"	1
			6½" x 2½"	1
			8½" x 2½"	1
	3½" x WOF	1	12½" x 3½"	1
Cactus	1½" x WOF	1	12½" x 1½"	2
	2½" x WOF	1	2½" x 2½"	1
			8½" x 2½"	1
			10½" x 2½"	1
			12½" x 2½"	1
Ice Frappe	2½" x WOF	1	2½" x 2½"	2
			4½" x 2½"	1
			6½" x 2½"	2

BLOCK 105: Half-Square Triangle – 2"

Strips	A: Snow-1339	2
	B: Olive-1263	1
	C: Candy Green-1061	1
	D: Cactus-199	1
	E: Ice Frappe-1173	1
Squares	A: Snow-1339	30
	B: Olive-1263	7
	C: Candy Green-1061	8
	D: Cactus-199	10
	E: Ice Frappe-1173	7
Combos	A/B	7
	A/C	7
	A/D	9
	A/E	7
	D/C	1
HST	A/B	14
	A/C	14
	A/D	18
	A/E	13
	D/C	2

APPENDIX A: i want that exact quilt

eco-parallel-esque

YARDAGE: Blocks & Setting

Aqua-1005	4⅜ yards	**Batting**	111" x 106"
Zucchini-354	1⅝ yards	**Backing:** Aqua-1005	9 yards
Salmon-1483	1½ yards		
Artichoke-347	1¾ yards	**Binding:** Mushroom-1239	1 yard (11 strips)
White-1387	4 yards		
Mushroom-1239	2⅛ yards		

Assembly

1. Cut and assemble the blocks listed in the Details chart (12 total) in the specified sizes. A combined cutting chart and block color assignments are below and assembly instructions are on p. 72.

2. Construct -esque, QUILT 103, following the cutting chart and instructions on p. 86 using colors **A:** Aqua-1005, **B:** Zucchini-354, **C:** Salmon-1483, **D:** Artichoke-347, **E:** White-1387, **F:** Mushroom-1239.

CUTTING: Blocks

	First Cut		Second Cut	
	Dimensions	Quantity	Dimensions	Quantity
White	1½" x WOF	26	1½" x 1½"	10
			5½" x 1½"	2
			6½" x 1½"	1
			10½" x 1½"	28
			12½" x 1½"	9
			13½" x 1½"	10
			16½" x 1½"	12
			17½" x 1½"	2
			18½" x 1½"	2
	4½" x WOF	4	6½" x 4½"	1
			12½" x 4½"	7
			18½" x 4½"	2
	6½" x WOF	1	12½" x 6½"	2
Artichoke	1½" x WOF	13	4½" x 1½"	1
			10½" x 1½"	23
			16½" x 1½"	8
Salmon	1½" x WOF	8	10½" x 1½"	14
			16½" x 1½"	6

details

COLOR	103 p. 37	eco	
		size	quantity
BLOCK	114 p. 72	6" x 6"◊	1
		6" x 12"◊	4
		12" x 12"◊	1
		12" x 18"◊	3
		12" x 24"◊	1
		18" x 18"◊	2
QUILT	103 p. 86	-esque 103" x 98"	

◊ finished size

block color assignments

BLOCK 114: -parallel
A: White-1387
B: Artichoke-347
C: Salmon-1483

paleo-domus-esque

YARDAGE: Blocks & Setting

Mushroom-1239	4⅜ yards	Cappuccino-406	¼ yard
Maize-1216	1¾ yards	**Batting**	111" x 106"
Dusty Blue-362	1⅝ yards	**Backing:** Dusty Blue-362	9 yards
Sunflower-353	1⅞ yards		
Snow-1339	3⅜ yards	**Binding:** Cappuccino-406	1 yard (11 strips)
Sky-1513	2⅝ yards		

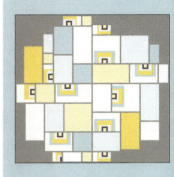

Assembly

1. Cut and assemble the blocks listed in the Details chart (12 total) in the specified sizes. A combined cutting chart and block color assignments are below and assembly instructions are on p. 58.

2. Construct -esque, QUILT 103, following the cutting chart and instructions on p. 86 using colors **A:** Mushroom-1239, **B:** Maize-1216, **C:** Dusty Blue-362, **D:** Sunflower-353, **E:** Snow-1339, **F:** Sky-1513.

details

COLOR	111 p. 41	paleo	
BLOCK	107 p. 58	size	quantity
		6" x 6" ϕ	1
		6" x 12" ϕ	4
		12" x 12" ϕ	1
		12" x 18" ϕ	3
		12" x 24" ϕ	1
		18" x 18" ϕ	2
QUILT	103 p. 86	-esque 103" x 98"	

ϕ finished size

block color assignments

BLOCK 107: -domus
A: Snow-1339
B: Dusty Blue-362
C: Sunflower-353
D: Sky-1513
E: Cappuccino-406
F: Maize-1216

CUTTING: Blocks

	First Cut		Second Cut	
	Dimensions	Quantity	Dimensions	Quantity
Snow	1½" x WOF	2	8½" x 1½"	6
	2½" x WOF	1	6½" x 2½"	1
			7½" x 2½"	1
	3½" x WOF	2	6½" x 3½"	4
			8½" x 3½"	5
	4½" x WOF	3	18½" x 4½"	3
			24½" x 4½"	1
	5½" x WOF	1	12½" x 5½"	1
	8½" x WOF	1	9½" x 8½"	1
	10½" x WOF	1	18½" x 10½"	2
Dusty Blue	1½" x WOF	3	14½" x 1½"	6
	2½" x WOF	3	7½" x 2½"	12
Sunflower	1½" x WOF	3	4½" x 1½"	19
	2½" x WOF	2	4½" x 2½"	1
			9½" x 2½"	4
	3½" x WOF	3	10½" x 3½"	7
Sky	1½" x WOF	3	3½" x 1½"	1
			8½" x 1½"	11
	2½" x WOF	3	3½" x 2½"	23
Cappuccino	1½" x WOF	3	2½" x 1½"	22
			3½" x 1½"	1
			4½" x 1½"	11
Maize	2½" x WOF	1	2½" x 2½"	11

APPENDIX A: i want that exact quilt

geo-macro-flora-mania

YARDAGE: Blocks & Setting

Sprout-254	1 yard	**Batting**	48" x 58"	
Oyster-1268	1⅞ yards	**Backing:**	2¾ yards	
Leprechaun-411	⅞ yard	Mango-192		
Mango-192	⅜ yard	**Binding:**	½ yard (5 strips)	
Chestnut-407	⅝ yard	Chestnut-407		

Assembly

1. Cut and assemble the blocks listed in the Details chart (6 total) in the specified sizes. A combined cutting chart and block color assignments are below and assembly instructions are on p. 48 (BLOCK 102) and p. 60 (BLOCK 108).

2. Construct -mania, QUILT 104, following the cutting chart and instructions on p. 92 using color A: Sprout-254.

details

		size	quantity
COLOR	105 p. 38	geo	
BLOCK	102 p. 48	12" x 18" ϕ	1
		12" x 24" ϕ	1
		18" x 18" ϕ	1
	108 p. 60	12" x 12" ϕ	1
		12" x 18" ϕ	1
		18" x 18" ϕ	1
QUILT	104 p. 52	-mania 40" x 50"	

ϕ finished size

block color assignments

BLOCK 102: -flora
A: Oyster-1268
B: Leprechaun-411
C: Sprout-254
D: Mango-192
E: Chestnut-407

BLOCK 108: -macro
A: Sprout-254
B: Oyster-1268
C: Mango-192
D: Leprechaun-411
E: Chestnut-407

CUTTING: Blocks

	First Cut		**Second Cut**	
	Dimensions	Quantity	Dimensions	Quantity
Oyster	1½" x WOF	3	12½" x 1½"	2
			16½" x 1½"	2
			18½" x 1½"	2
	2½" x WOF	2	2½" x 2½"	8
			4½" x 2½"	4
			18½" x 2½"	1
	4½" x WOF	1	3½" x 4½"	4
			4½" x 4½"	1
	7½" x WOF	1	7½" x 12½"	2
	8½" x WOF	1	4½" x 8½"	2
			7½" x 8½"	2
			8½" x 8½"	1
Chestnut	2½" x WOF	1	2½" x 2½"	4
Leprechaun	2½" x WOF	1	2½" x 2½"	8

BLOCKS 102 & 108: Quarter Curve – 2"

Strips	Sprout-254	2
	Oyster-1268	8
	Mango-192	4
	Leprechaun-411	6
	Chestnut-407	5
Curves ‡	Sprout-254	20**i**
	Oyster-1268	88**o**, 36**i**
	Mango-192	24**o**, 38**i**
	Leprechaun-411	36**o**, 54**i**
	Chestnut-407	36**o**, 36**i**
Combos: Block 102	A/B	18
	A/C	8
	A/D	14
	A/E	16
Combos: Block 108	B/A	12
	B/E	20
	C/B	24
	D/B	12
	D/C	24
	E/D	36

‡ Inner (**i**)/Outer (**o**) Curves

BLOCK 102: Half-Square Triangle – 2"

Strips	A: Oyster-1268	1
	B: Leprechaun-411	1
Squares	A: Oyster-1268	8
	B: Leprechaun-411	8
†	A/B	8
HST	A/B	16

† Combos

130 color, block & quilt

luma-tele-asaurus

YARDAGE: Blocks & Setting

Iron-408	½ yard	Bone-1037	2⅜ yards
Citrus-1077	1⅝ yards	Batting	94" x 92"
Peapod-414	1¼ yards	Backing: Iron-408	7¾ yards
Charcoal-1071	1¼ yards		
Ash-1007	½ yard	Binding: Charcoal-1071	¾ yards (9 strips)
White-1387	2 yards		

Assembly

1. Cut and assemble the blocks listed in the Details chart (11 total) in the specified sizes. A combined cutting chart and block color assignments are below and assembly instructions are on p. 62.

2. Construct -asaurus, QUILT 105, following the cutting chart and instructions on p. 96 using colors A: Bone-1037, B: Peapod-414, C: Citrus-1077, D: Charcoal-1071.

CUTTING: Blocks

BLOCK 109: Half-Square Triangle – 3"

Strips	A: Iron-408	4
	B: Citrus-1077	3
	C: Peapod-414	3
	D: Charcoal-1071	3
	E: Ash-1007	4
	F: White-1387	17
Squares	A: Iron-408	44
	B: Citrus-1077	28
	C: Peapod-414	33
	D: Charcoal-1071	33
	E: Ash-1007	39
	F: White-1387	177
Combos	A/F	44
	B/F	28
	C/F	33
	D/F	33
	E/F	39
HST	A/F	88
	B/F	55
	C/F	66
	D/F	66
	E/F	77

details

COLOR	109 p. 40	luma	
		size	quantity
BLOCK	109 p. 62	12" x 24" ⁕	11
QUILT	105 p. 96	-asaurus 86" x 84"	

⁕ finished size

block color assignments

BLOCK 109: -tele
A: Iron-408
B: Citrus-1077
C: Peapod-414
D: Charcoal-1071
E: Ash-1007
F: White-1387

APPENDIX A: i want that exact quilt

trans-poly-asaurus

YARDAGE: Blocks & Setting

Parchment-413	2⅜ yards	Iron-408	½ yard
Olive-1263	2 yards	**Batting**	94" x 92"
Corn Yellow-1089	1⅜ yards	**Backing:** Parchment-413	7¾ yards
Amber-1479	1¾ yards		
Mushroom-1239	2¾ yards	**Binding:** Mushroom-1239	¾ yards (9 strips)
Bone-1037	2⅜ yards		

Assembly

1. Cut and assemble the blocks listed in the Details chart (11 total) in the specified sizes. A combined cutting chart is below and the opposite page, block color assignments are below and assembly instructions are on p. 50 (BLOCK 103), p. 52 (BLOCK 104), p. 62 (BLOCK 109) and p. 66 (BLOCK 111).

2. Construct -asaurus, QUILT 105, following the cutting chart and instructions on p. 96 using colors A: Parchment-413, B: Olive-1263, C: Corn Yellow-1089, D: Amber-1479.

CUTTING: Blocks

	First Cut		Second Cut	
	Dimensions	**Quantity**	**Dimensions**	**Quantity**
Mushroom	2½" x WOF	2	2½" x 2½"	6
			4½" x 2½"	6
	3½" x WOF	4	24½" x 3½"	4
	5½" x WOF	2	12½" x 5½"	6
Amber	2½" x WOF	4	1½" x 2½"	15
			2½" x 2½"	35
			3½" x 2½"	3
			4½" x 2½"	3
Iron	4½" x WOF	1	4½" x 4½"	2
Corn Yellow	4½" x WOF	1	4½" x 4½"	2
Olive	2½" x WOF	4	1½" x 2½"	15
			2½" x 2½"	35
			3½" x 2½"	3
			4½" x 2½"	3
	4½" x WOF	1	4½" x 4½"	2
Bone	1½" x WOF	2	4½" x 1½"	4
			14½" x 1½"	4
	2½" x WOF	1	2½" x 2½"	6
			6½" x 2½"	2
	6½" x WOF	1	8½" x 6½"	2

details

COLOR	107 p. 39	trans	
		size	quantity
BLOCK	103 p. 50	12" x 24" ⬦	4
	104 p. 52	12" x 24" ⬦	3
	109 p. 62	12" x 24" ⬦	2
	111 p. 66	12" x 24" ⬦	2
QUILT	105 p. 96	-asaurus 86" x 84"	

⬦ finished size

block color assignments

BLOCK 103: -rumpo
A: Mushroom-1239
B: Bone-1037
C: Amber-1479
D: Olive-1263

BLOCK 104: -pluvia
A: Mushroom-1239
B: Amber-1479
C: Olive-1263
D: Bone-1037

BLOCK 109: -tele
A: Amber-1479
B: Olive-1263
C: Iron-408
D: Mushroom-1239
E: Corn Yellow-1089
F: Bone-1037

BLOCK 111: -insta
A: Mushroom-1239
B: Bone-1037
C: Iron-408
D: Corn Yellow-1089
E: Olive-1263

BLOCKS 103 & 104: Quarter Curve – 2"

Strips	Mushroom-1239	16
	Bone-1037	15
	Amber-1479	2
	Olive-1263	2
Curves †	Mushroom-1239	236**o**
	Bone-1037	236**i**
	Amber-1479	6**o**, 6**i**
	Olive-1263	6**o**, 6**i**
‡	A/B	224
Combos: BLOCK 104	A/B	6
	A/C	6
	B/D	6
	C/D	6

† Inner (**i**)/Outer (**o**) Curves
‡ Combos: BLOCK 103

BLOCK 104: Half-Square Triangle – 2"

Strips	A: Mushroom-1239	1
	B: Amber-1479	1
	C: Olive-1263	1
	D: Bone-1037	1
Squares	A: Mushroom-1239	12
	B: Amber-1479	9
	C: Olive-1263	9
	D: Bone-1037	6
Combos	A/B	6
	A/C	6
	B/D	3
	C/D	3
HST	A/B	12
	A/C	12
	B/D	6
	C/D	6

BLOCK 109: Half-Square Triangle – 3"

Strips	A: Amber-1479	1
	B: Olive-1263	1
	C: Iron-408	1
	D: Mushroom-1239	1
	E: Corn Yellow-1089	1
	F: Bone-1037	3
Squares	A: Amber-1479	8
	B: Olive-1263	5
	C: Iron-408	6
	D: Mushroom-1239	6
	E: Corn Yellow-1089	7
	F: Bone-1037	32
Combos	A/F	8
	B/F	5
	C/F	6
	D/F	6
	E/F	7
HST	A/F	16
	B/F	10
	C/F	12
	D/F	12
	E/F	14

APPENDIX A: i want that exact quilt

aqua-codex-athon

YARDAGE: Blocks & Setting

Bone-1037	3 yards	Dusty Blue-362	¼ yard
Jade Green-1183	⅞ yard	Batting	68" x 78"
Candy Green-1061	⅞ yard	Backing: Aqua-1005	3⅞ yards
Aqua-1005	¾ yard		
Pond-200	1 yard	Binding: Jade Green-1183	⅝ yards (7 strips)
Caribbean-1064	½ yard		

Assembly

1. Cut and assemble the blocks listed in the Details chart (3 total) in the specified sizes. A combined cutting chart and block color assignments are below and assembly instructions are on p. 74.

2. Construct -athon, QUILT 107, following the cutting chart and instructions on p. 104 using colors **A:** Bone-1037, **B:** Jade Green-1183, **C:** Candy Green-1061, **D:** Aqua-1005, **E:** Pond-200, **F:** Caribbean-1064.

CUTTING: Blocks

	First Cut		Second Cut	
	Dimensions	Quantity	Dimensions	Quantity
Bone	2½" x WOF	4	2½" x 2½"	12
			4½" x 2½"	11
			8½" x 2½"	2
			10½" x 2½"	1
			12½" x 2½"	1
			14½" x 2½"	2
	4½" x WOF	3	4½" x 4½"	1
			6½" x 4½"	1
			12½" x 4½"	3
			18½" x 4½"	2
Aqua	2½" x WOF	1	2½" x 2½"	16
Jade Green	2½" x WOF	1	2½" x 2½"	14
Pond	2½" x WOF	1	2½" x 2½"	12
Dusty Blue	2½" x WOF	1	2½" x 2½"	9
Candy Green	2½" x WOF	1	2½" x 2½"	16

details

COLOR	104 p. 37	aqua	
		size	quantity
BLOCK	115 p. 43	12" x 18" ⬥	1
		18" x 18" ⬥	2
QUILT	107 p. 104	-athon 60" x 70"	

⬥ finished size

block color assignments

BLOCK 115: -codex
A: Bone-1037
B: Aqua-1005
C: Jade Green-1183
D: Pond-200
E: Dusty Blue-362
F: Candy Green-1061

color, block & quilt

florus-orbis-athon

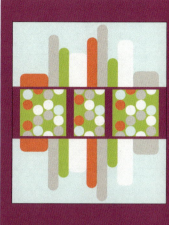

YARDAGE: Blocks & Setting

Kumquat-410	⅞ yard	Batting	68" x 78"
Stone-1362	1⅛ yards	Backing: Stone-1362	3⅞ yards
Ice Frappe-1173	2⅜ yards		
White-1387	1⅛ yards	Binding: Cerise-1066	⅝ yards (7 strips)
Peapod-414	1⅞ yards		
Cerise-1066	½ yard		

Assembly

1. Cut and assemble the blocks listed in the Details chart (3 total) in the specified sizes. A combined cutting chart and block color assignments are below and assembly instructions are on p. 46.

2. Construct -athon, QUILT 107, following the cutting chart and instructions on p. 104 using colors A: Ice Frappe-1173, B: Kumquat-410, C: Stone-1362, D: Peapod-414, E: White-1387, F: Cerise-1066.

CUTTING: Blocks

	First Cut		Second Cut	
	Dimensions	Quantity	Dimensions	Quantity
Peapod	1½" x WOF	2	18½" x 1½"	4
	4½" x WOF	2	4½" x 4½"	11

BLOCK 101: Quarter Curve – 2"

Strips	A: Peapod-414	10
	B: White-1387	3
	C: Stone-1362	4
	D: Kumquat-410	2
	E: Ice Frappe-1173	2
†	A: Peapod-414	154**o**
	B: White-1387	44**i**
	C: Stone-1362	50**i**
	D: Kumquat-410	28**i**
	E: Ice Frappe-1173	32**i**
Combos	A/B	44
	A/C	50
	A/D	28
	A/E	32

† Inner (**i**)/Outer (**o**) Curves

details

COLOR	108 p. 39	florus	
		size	quantity
BLOCK	101 p. 46	12"x 18"ϕ	1
		18"x 18"ϕ	2
QUILT	107 p. 104	-athon 60"x 70"	

ϕ finished size

block color assignments

BLOCK 101: -orbis
A: Peapod-414
B: White-1387
C: Stone-1362
D: Kumquat-410
E: Ice Frappe-1173

APPENDIX A: i want that exact quilt

lapis-curva-ism

YARDAGE: Blocks & Setting

Cerise-1066	⅝ yard	Lapis-357	½ yard	
✓ Wisteria-1392	⅞ yard	Batting	58" x 58"	
✓ Dark Violet-1485	1⅛ yards	Backing: Dark Violet-1485	3⅜ yards	} 1 yd
✓ Lavender-1189	⅝ yard			
Ash-1007	¾ yard	Binding: Lapis-357	½ yard (6 strips)	
✓ Tulip-327	1⅛ yards			

Assembly

1. Cut and assemble the blocks listed in the Details chart (3 total) in the specified sizes. A combined cutting chart and block color assignments are below and assembly instructions are on p. 70.

2. Construct -ism, QUILT 108, following the cutting chart and instructions on p. 110 using colors ■ **A:** Tulip-327, ■ **B:** Wisteria-1392, ■ **C:** Dark Violet-1485, ■ **D:** Lavender-1189, ■ **E:** Lapis-357, ■ **F:** Ash-1007.

details

		size	quantity
COLOR	114 p. 42	lapis	
BLOCK	113 p. 70	6" x 12" ◊	1
		12" x 12" ◊	1
		12" x 24" ◊	1
QUILT	108 p. 110	-ism 50" x 50"	

◊ finished size

block color assignments

BLOCK 113: -curva
- **A:** Wisteria-1392
- **B:** Lavender-1189
- **C:** Cerise-1066
- **D:** Dark Violet-1485
- **E:** Ash-1007
- **F:** Tulip-327

CUTTING: Blocks

	First Cut		Second Cut	
	Dimensions	Quantity	Dimensions	Quantity
Cerise	3½" x WOF	2	3½" x 3½"	4
			9½" x 3½"	4

BLOCK 113: Quarter Curve – 3"

Strips	A: Wisteria-1392	2
	B: Lavender-1189	2
	C: Cerise-1066	2
	D: Dark Violet-1485	1
	E: Ash-1007	2
	F: Tulip-327	2
Inner (i)/Outer (o) Curves	A: Wisteria-1392	12o, 6i
	B: Lavender-1189	2o, 12i
	C: Cerise-1066	4o, 8i
	D: Dark Violet-1485	8o, 2i
	E: Ash-1007	6o, 8i
	F: Tulip-327	8o, 4i
Combos	A/B	4
	A/C	4
	A/E	4
	B/D	2
	C/A	4
	D/A	2
	D/B	2
	D/C	4
	E/B	2
	F/F	4
	F/B	4
	F/E	4

inter-proto-ism

YARDAGE: Blocks & Setting

Putty-1303	¾ yard	Oyster-1268	¾ yard
Parchment-413	⅜ yard	**Batting**	58" x 58"
Cheddar-350	½ yard	**Backing:** Sprout-254	3⅜ yards
Kumquat-410	1⅛ yards		
Peach-1281	¾ yard	**Binding:** Parchment-413	½ yard (6 strips)
Sprout-254	½ yard		

Assembly

1. Cut and assemble the blocks listed in the Details chart (3 total) in the specified sizes. A combined cutting chart and block color assignments are below and assembly instructions are on p. 68.

2. Construct -ism, QUILT 108, following the cutting chart and instructions on p. 110 using colors **A:** Putty-1303, **B:** Peach-1281, **C:** Kumquat-410, **D:** Cheddar-350, **E:** Sprout-254, **F:** Parchment-413.

CUTTING: Blocks

	First Cut		Second Cut	
	Dimensions	Quantity	Dimensions	Quantity
Oyster	1½" x WOF	14	1½" x 1½"	23
			2½" x 1½"	11
			3½" x 1½"	8
			4½" x 1½"	12
			5½" x 1½"	6
			6½" x 1½"	11
			7½" x 1½"	9
			8½" x 1½"	11
			9½" x 1½"	6
			10½" x 1½"	1
Peach	1½" x WOF	3	1½" x 1½"	19
			2½" x 1½"	1
			3½" x 1½"	1
			4½" x 1½"	2
			8½" x 1½"	2
			9½" x 1½"	2
Kumquat	1½" x WOF	3	1½" x 1½"	19
			2½" x 1½"	1
			3½" x 1½"	1
			4½" x 1½"	2
			8½" x 1½"	2
			9½" x 1½"	2
Cheddar	1½" x WOF	3	1½" x 1½"	19
			2½" x 1½"	1
			3½" x 1½"	1
			4½" x 1½"	2
			8½" x 1½"	2
			9½" x 1½"	2

details

		size	quantity
COLOR	113 p. 42	inter	
BLOCK	112 p. 68	6" x 12"ϕ	1
		12" x 12"ϕ	1
		12" x 24"ϕ	1
QUILT	108 p. 110	-ism 50" x 50"	

ϕ finished size

block color assignments

BLOCK 112: -proto
A: Oyster-1268
B: Peach-1281
C: Kumquat-410
D: Cheddar-350

APPENDIX A: i want that exact quilt

lux-curva-ette

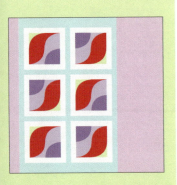

details

COLOR	115 p. 43	lux	
BLOCK		size	quantity
	113 p. 70	6" x 6" ⌀	6
QUILT	109 p. 114	-ette 30" x 30"	

⌀ finished size

block color assignments

BLOCK 113: -curva
- **A:** Lipstick-1194
- **C:** Thistle-134
- **D:** Honey Dew-21
- **E:** Wisteria-1392

YARDAGE: Blocks & Setting

	Petunia-24	½ yard		Wisteria-1392	¼ yard
	Aqua-1005	⅜ yard		**Batting**	38" x 38"
	White-1387	⅜ yard		**Backing:** Aqua-1005	1⅛ yards
	Honey Dew-21	¼ yard			
	Lipstick-1194	⅜ yard		**Binding:** Wisteria-1392	⅜ yards (4 strips)
	Thistle-134	⅜ yard			

Assembly

1. Cut and assemble the blocks listed in the Details chart (6 total) in the specified sizes. A combined cutting chart and block color assignments are below and assembly instructions are on p. 70.

2. Construct -ette, QUILT 109, following the cutting chart and instructions on p. 114 using colors **A:** Petunia-24, **B:** Aqua-1005, **C:** White-1387.

CUTTING: Blocks

	BLOCK 113: Quarter Curve – 3"	
Strips	**A:** Lipstick-1194	2
	C: Thistle-134	2
	D: Honey Dew-21	1
	E: Wisteria-1392	1
†	**A:** Lipstick-1194	6**o**, 12**i**
	C: Thistle-134	12**o**, 6**i**
	D: Honey Dew-21	6**o**
	E: Wisteria-1392	6**i**
Combos	A/C	6
	C/A	6
	C/E	6
	D/A	6

† Inner (**i**)/Outer (**o**) Curves

nano-poly-ette

YARDAGE: Blocks & Setting

Poppy-1296	½ yard	Cactus-199	⅜ yard	
Mango-192	⅜ yard	Batting	38" x 38"	
Chartreuse-1072	⅜ yard	Backing:	1⅛ yards	
Pomegranate-1295	½ yard	Kumquat-410		
Papaya-149	¼ yard	Binding:	⅜ yards (4 strips)	
White-1387	⅜ yard	Papaya-149		
Kumquat-410	⅜ yard			

details

		size	quantity
COLOR	112 p. 41	nano	
BLOCK	106 p. 56	6"x 6" ϕ	1
	107 p. 58	6"x 6" ϕ	1
	109 p. 62	6"x 6" ϕ	1
	111 p. 66	6"x 6" ϕ	1
	114 p. 72	6"x 6" ϕ	1
	115 p. 74	6"x 6" ϕ	1
QUILT	109 p. 114	-ette	30" x 30"

ϕ finished size

Assembly

1. Cut and assemble the blocks listed in the Details chart (6 total) in the specified sizes. A combined cutting chart and block color assignments are below and assembly instructions are on p. 56 (BLOCK 106), p. 58 (BLOCK 107), p. 62 (BLOCK 109), p. 66 (BLOCK 111), p. 72 (BLOCK 114) and p. 74 (BLOCK 115).

2. Construct -ette, QUILT 109, following the cutting chart and instructions on p. 114 using colors A: Pomegranate-1295, B: Kumquat-410, C: Cactus-199.

CUTTING: Blocks

	First Cut		Second Cut	
	Dimensions	Quantity	Dimensions	Quantity
Poppy	1½" x WOF	1	1½" x 1½"	2
			3½" x 1½"	1
			6½" x 1½"	1
	2½" x WOF	1	3½" x 2½"	1
			5½" x 2½"	1
	4½" x WOF	1	6½" x 4½"	1
Mango	2½" x WOF	1	2½" x 2½"	2
			6½" x 2½"	1
	4½" x WOF	1	4½" x 1½"	1
			4½" x 3½"	1
Chartreuse	1½" x WOF	1	4½" x 1½"	1
	2½" x WOF	1	2½" x 2½"	1
			4½" x 2½"	1
			6½" x 2½"	1
Papaya	2½" x WOF	1	2½" x 2½"	1
White	1½" x WOF	1	2½" x 1½"	1
			3½" x 1½"	4
			5½" x 1½"	1
			6½" x 1½"	2
	2½" x WOF	1	2½" x 2½"	3
			3½" x 2½"	1
			6½" x 2½"	1

BLOCK 109: Half-Square Triangle – 3"

Strips	A: Chartreuse-1072	1
	B: Poppy-1296	1
	C: Papaya-149	1
	D: Mango-192	1
	F: White-1387	1
Squares	A: Chartreuse-1072	1
	B: Poppy-1296	1
	C: Papaya-149	1
	D: Mango-192	1
	F: White-1387	4
Combos	A/F	1
	B/F	1
	C/F	1
	D/F	1
HST	A/F	1
	B/F	1
	C/F	1
	D/F	1

block color assignments

BLOCK 106: -auto
A: White-1387
B: Mango-192
C: Poppy-1296

BLOCK 107: -domus
A: Mango-192
C: Chartreuse-1072
D: White-1387
E: Poppy-1296

BLOCK 109: -tele
A: Chartreuse-1072
B: Poppy-1296
C: Papaya-149
D: Mango-192
F: White-1387

BLOCK 111: -insta
A: Chartreuse-1072
B: White-1387
C: Mango-192

BLOCK 114: -parallel
A: Poppy-1296
B: Mango-192

BLOCK 115: -codex
A: White-1387
C: Mango-192
E: Papaya-149
F: Chartreuse-1072

APPENDIX A: i want that exact quilt

circum-poly-avore

YARDAGE: Blocks & Setting

	Ivory-1181	1 yard		**Batting**	39" x 48"
	Pond-200	½ yards		**Backing:** Pond-200	1⅜ yards
	Tangerine-1370	¼ yard			
	Dusty Peach-1465	⅛ yard		**Binding:** Tangerine-1370	⅜ yards (4 strips)
	Corn Yellow-1089	⅛ yard			
	Azure-1009	1¾ yards			

Assembly

1. Cut and assemble the blocks listed in the Details chart (5 total) in the specified sizes. A combined cutting chart and block color assignments are below and assembly instructions are on p. 48 (BLOCK 102), p. 60 (BLOCK 108) and p. 64 (BLOCK 110).

2. Construct -avore, QUILT 110, following the cutting chart and instructions on p. 118 using color A: Azure-1009.

details

		size	quantity
COLOR	102 p. 36	circum	
BLOCK	102 p. 48	6"x 6" ϕ	1
		12"x 18" ϕ	1
	108 p. 60	6"x 6" ϕ	1
	110 p. 64	6"x 12" ϕ	2
QUILT	110 p. 118	-avore 31"x 40"	

ϕ finished size

block color assignments

BLOCK 102: -flora
A: Ivory-1181
B: Pond-200
C: Corn Yellow-1089
D: Dusty Peach-1465
E: Tangerine-1370

BLOCK 108: -macro
A: Corn Yellow-1089
B: Tangerine-1370
C: Ivory-1181
D: Pond-200
E: Dusty Peach

BLOCK 110: -retro
A: Ivory-1181
B: Pond-200
C: Tangerine-1370

CUTTING: Blocks

	First Cut		**Second Cut**	
	Dimensions	Quantity	Dimensions	Quantity
Ivory	1½" x WOF	2	12½" x 1½"	4
	2½" x WOF	1	2½" x 2½"	1
			4½" x 2½"	4
	4½" x WOF	1	3½" x 4½"	2
	7½" x WOF	1	7½" x 8½"	2
Pond	2½" x WOF	1	2½" x 2½"	3
Dusty Peach	2½" x WOF	1	2½" x 2½"	1

BLOCK 102: Half-Square Triangle – 2"

	A: Ivory-1181	1
Strips	B: Pond-200	1
Squares	A: Ivory-1181	4
	B: Pond-200	4
*	A/B	4
**	A/B	7

* Combos
** HST

BLOCKS 102, 108 & 110: Quarter Curve – 2"

Strips	Ivory-1181	2
	Pond-200	2
	Corn Yellow-1089	1
	Dusty Peach-1465	1
	Tangerine-1370	2
Curves †	Ivory-1181	28o, 2i
	Pond-200	3o, 22i
	Corn Yellow-1089	3i
	Dusty Peach-1465	2o, 4i
	Tangerine-1370	9o, 11i
Combos: BLOCK 102	A/B	4
	A/C	2
	A/D	4
	A/E	8
Combos: BLOCK 108	B/A	1
	C/B	2
	D/B	1
	D/C	2
	E/D	2
‡	A/B	8
	C/B	8

† Inner (**i**)/Outer (**o**) Curves
‡ Combos: BLOCK 110

TOP: terra-pluvia-scope
terra, COLOR 101, p. 36
-pluvia, BLOCK 104, p. 52
-scope, QUILT 106, p. 100
APPENDIX, p. 125

BOTTOM LEFT: geo-macro-flora-mania
geo, COLOR 105, p. 38
-flora, BLOCK 102, p. 48
-macro, BLOCK 108, p. 60
-mania, QUILT 104, p. 92
APPENDIX, p. 130

BOTTOM RIGHT: circum-poly-avore
circum, COLOR 102, p. 36
-flora, BLOCK 102, p. 48
-macro, BLOCK 108, p. 60
-retro, BLOCK 110, p. 64
-avore, QUILT 110, p. 118
APPENDIX, p. 140

APPENDIX A: i want that exact quilt

APPENDIX B:
Where in Washington

One of the best parts of this project was scouring hiking books and finding beautiful spots to take pictures while exploring with the family. Curious where a picture was taken? This list has it all.

page	location	city, WA
cover	Griffiths-Priday State Park	Copalis Beach
2	Deception Pass State Park	Fidalgo Island
3	Griffiths-Priday State Park	Copalis Beach
4	along the Wenatchee River	Stevens Pass
5	Griffiths-Priday State Park	Copalis Beach
6	Deception Pass State Park	Fidalgo Island
7	along the Nisqually River	Mount Rainier National Park
8	Alki Beach Park	Seattle
9	Mount Rainier National Park	Paradise
10	Deception Pass State Park	Fidalgo Island
29	Lincoln Park	Seattle
30	Paradise	Mount Rainier National Park
31	Jack Block Park	Seattle
32	Woodland Park Rose Garden	Seattle
36 TOP	Paradise	Mount Rainier National Park
36 BOTTOM	My Backyard	Seattle

page	location	city, WA
37 TOP	along the Strait of Juan de Fuca	Clallam Bay
37 BOTTOM	Alki Beach Park	Seattle
38 TOP	Woodland Park Rose Garden	Seattle
38 BOTTOM	Cape Flattery	Neah Bay
39 TOP	Hoh Rain Forest	Olympic National Park
39 BOTTOM	Ohme Gardens	Wenatchee
40 TOP	Woodland Park Rose Garden	Seattle
40 BOTTOM	Deception Pass State Park	Fidalgo Island
41 TOP	Griffiths-Priday State Park	Copalis Beach
41 BOTTOM	My Backyard	Seattle
42 BOTTOM	Woodland Park Rose Garden	Seattle
43	Paradise	Mount Rainier National Park
44	Griffiths-Priday State Park	Copalis Beach
46, 47	Deception Pass State Park	Fidalgo Island
48	Deception Pass State Park	Fidalgo Island

page	location	city, WA
52	Griffiths-Priday State Park	Copalis Beach
56	Alki Beach Park	Seattle
59	Lincoln Park	Seattle
61	Luna Park Pier	Seattle
63	Lincoln Park	Seattle
64, 65	Griffiths-Priday State Park	Copalis Beach
66	along Harbor Avenue	Seattle
67	Griffiths-Priday State Park	Copalis Beach
70	Deception Pass State Park	Fidalgo Island
73	Ebey's Landing	Whidbey Island
75	Paradise	Mount Rainier National Park
76	Deception Pass State Park	Fidalgo Island
78	Paradise	Mount Rainier National Park
79	Griffiths-Priday State Park	Copalis Beach
82	along the Nisqually River	Mount Rainier National Park
83	Ebey's Landing	Whidbey Island
86	Ebey's Landing	Whidbey Island
87	Lincoln Park	Seattle
92	Luna Park Pier	Seattle
93	Deception Pass State Park	Fidalgo Island
95	Deception Pass State Park	Fidalgo Island
96	Griffiths-Priday State Park	Copalis Beach
97	Lincoln Park	Seattle
99	along Harbor Avenue	Seattle
100, 101	Griffiths-Priday State Park	Copalis Beach
103	Griffiths-Priday State Park	Copalis Beach
104	along the Nisqually River	Mount Rainier National Park
105	Deception Pass State Park	Fidalgo Island
107	along the Nisqually River	Mount Rainier National Park
108	along the Nisqually River	Mount Rainier National Park
110	Ebey's Landing	Whidbey Island
111	Griffiths-Priday State Park	Copalis Beach
113	Griffiths-Priday State Park	Copalis Beach
114	Jack Block Park	Seattle
115	Deception Pass State Park	Fidalgo Island
117	Jack Block Park	Seattle
118	Ebey's Landing	Whidbey Island
119	Deception Pass State Park	Fidalgo Island
121	Ebey's Landing	Whidbey Island
122	Griffiths-Priday State Park	Copalis Beach
133	along Harbor Avenue	Seattle
141 TOP	Griffiths-Priday State Park	Copalis Beach
141 BOTTOM LEFT AND RIGHT	Deception Pass State Park	Fidalgo Island
142	Seacrest Pier	Seattle
144	along the Hoh River	Olympic National Park
145	Cape Flattery	Neah Bay
146	Griffiths-Priday State Park	Copalis Beach
back cover TOP	along the Nisqually River	Mount Rainier National Park
back cover BOTTOM	Griffiths-Priday State Park	Copalis Beach

APPENDIX B: where in washington

About the Author

Emily Cier desires only to live a normal life with her family in the Pacific Northwest. In order to achieve this goal, she must first rid herself of the plague of quilt designs, block ideas, shape concepts, and color palettes that invade her dreams, seep into her every waking hour, and deny her a moment's peace. Perhaps someday she will have satisfied the quilting spirits by translating all these ideas to concrete form. Until that day, she continues her daily toils to transcribe page after page of charts and illustrations.

Carolina Patchworks began as a way to fund Emily's fabric habit by selling the quilts she crafted, but has evolved over the years. Today, Carolina Patchworks has over 60 patterns in print, and including the tome you are holding in your hands, has penned four books on quilting. We can assure you, however, that there's more awesomeness yet to come.

For more of Emily's work, visit www.carolinapatchworks.com.

about the author

Resources

Kona Cotton Solids by Robert Kaufman Fabrics

Visit **robertkaufman.com** to see the complete Kona Cotton Solid range, purchase a color card and search for local and online fabric shops carrying Robert Kaufman fabrics.

Longarm Quilting by Angela Walters

Visit **quiltingismytherapy.com** for more information on Angela, her quilting, classes and books.

above: behind the scenes of the QUILT 108 photo on p. 113. Maeve and Liam working together to hold the quilt straight in crazy coastal winds on Copalis Beach.

Architects need blueprints. Writers need drafts. Quilters crafting a creation from COLOR, BLOCK & QUILT need the WORKBOOK. Well, you don't *need* it, strictly speaking, but it sure could help to have a paper model of the quilt you're going to make in order to get it *just perfect* before you put thread to fabric, couldn't it? Besides, how often do you have such a good excuse to haul out that paste and scissors and play with miniatures? All the other quilters will be jealous — and you'll be spoiled for the next time you want to create a quilt that doesn't have a WORKBOOK!

Available at shop.carolinapatchworks.com.

Made in the USA
Charleston, SC
12 April 2013